2's Dramatic Play EXPERIENCE

Dress Up and Pretend!

2'S Dramatic Play EXPERIENCE

by
Liz & Dick Wilmes

Illustrations by
Janet McDonnell

A **BUILDING BLOCKS** Publication

38W567 Brindlewood, Elgin, Illinois 60123

ART

Cover Design and Graphics: David VanDelinder
                              STUDIO 155
                              Elgin, Illinois

Computer Graphics: Arlene Fiebig
                              PAPER PUSHERS
                              Darien, Wisconsin

Text Graphics: Janet McDonnell
                              Early Childhood Illustrator
                              Arlington Heights, Illinois

SPECIAL THANKS TO:
Cheryl Luppino and Mary Schuring for sharing so many ideas, activities, and special hints, so we can all help young children, get even more involved in their dramatic play.

Jeanne Lybecker for taking special care to compile the BOOK LIST. Now our young children can enjoy a great variety of books, as they pretend to be fire fighters, bus drivers, doctors, grocers, and more.

PUBLISHED BY:

38W567 Brindlewood
Elgin, Illinois 60123

ISBN 0-943452-20-1

Dedicated to teachers, who encourage very young children to "pretend and make believe."

CONTENTS

DRESS UP & PRETEND

AT THE BEACH

SET UP

Place

In the block center and other open spaces of your inside area and/or near the water faucet, but away from the general play space of your outside area.

Inside Setting

1. Put a small plastic pool to one side of the block area.

2. Have beach props, such as sun hats, beach bags, and adult bathing suits, on a shelf.

3. Place the full-length mirror near the bathing suits.

4. Have empty bottles of sun lotion and sun screen in a small basket.

5. In another open space have a sun bathing area. Put up a beach umbrella with low beach chairs. Have towels and a toy radio nearby.

Outside Setting

1. Hook up the hose. Turn on the water so that it trickles out of the nozzle.

2. Set the beach umbrella, low beach chairs, and towels near the hose.

3. Have several beachballs.

PROPS

Empty lotion bottles
Low beach chairs
Beach/vacation posters
Several wind-up radios
Full-length mirror
Beach bags
Beach towels
Beachballs
Small plastic pool
Beach umbrella
Hose

CLOTHES

Adult bathing suits
Swim caps
Sun glasses
Flip-flops
Sun hats
Child-size life preservers and rings
Swim goggles

PREPARATION

None

PLAY OPPORTUNITIES

1. **Play In the Sand.** Put sand in your sand table. Wet down the sand so that it is easy to mold, shovel, and dig. Have beach accessories available:

   ♦ Pails and shovels

   ♦ Sand blocks and molds

   ♦ Ice cube trays

   ♦ Scoops

   ♦ Muffin tins

   HINT: Have a spray bottle filled with water to keep the sand moist.

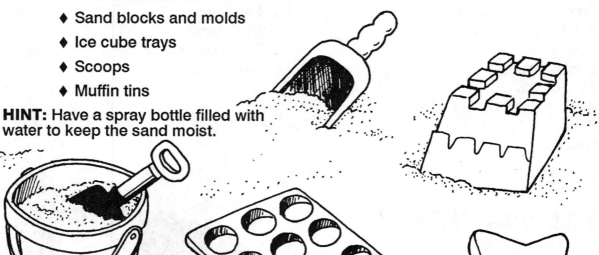

2. **Build Sand Castles.** Get a tall, narrow, unbreakable container, like a plastic glass, hollow block, or pitcher. Fill the container with sand, pack it down, and dump it over in the sand to form a castle. Do this over and over again. The children love to come along and slowly smash the castles down.

3. **Mid-Winter Beach Party.** Have the children get ready for the beach party by:

- ◆ Putting on adult swim suits over their clothes
- ◆ Taking off their shoes and putting on flip-flops or other beach shoes
- ◆ Putting their sun glasses, sun hats, beach towels, etc. in beach bags.

When the children get to the beach they can:

- ◆ Spread their beach towels and lay in the sun
- ◆ Play in the pool
- ◆ Put on life preservers and swim in the pool
- ◆ Listen to the radio while "sunning."

4. **Roll the Beachball.** Sit with the children and slowly roll the ball back and forth.

EXTENSION: After the "beach" has been put away, take out the parachute and roll the beachball back and forth and around the parachute.

5. **Sprinkler Day.** Attach the sprinkler to the hose. Have the children put on their bathing suits and swim shoes. Let them enjoy the water spraying out of the sprinkler.

HINT: Have adults walk with children through the sprinkler until they become comfortable with spraying water.

6. **Adult** "encourages" the beach play by being available to help the children:

- ◆ Put on bathing suits when needed
- ◆ Build sand castles
- ◆ Become comfortable with the sprinkler
- ◆ Tie shoes after swimming or sun bathing.

AT THE OFFICE

Place

In a large open area in the room.

Setting

1. Put two rectangular tables end-to-end. Set a few chairs around the tables.
2. Place a variety of props on the tables.
3. Hang the clothes on hooks near the tables.

PROPS

Old calculators (no batteries or cords)
Computer keyboards (cut cords)
Old typewriters
Telephones
Intercoms
Stamp pads and stamps
Scale to weigh letters
Old envelops
Heavy-weight paper
Greeting cards
Library pockets and cards
Carbonless paper tablets
Colored markers
Primary pencils
Colored pencils
Soft-sided briefcases
Old mailbags

CLOTHES

Letter carrier shirts
Letter carrier hats

PREPARATION

1. **Collect Heavyweight Paper.** Print shops often have excess paper in all weights, colors, and sizes. Contact a printer in your area and ask him/her to save heavyweight paper, card stock, envelops, and carbonless paper. Set a date and time to pick it up.

2. **Cut the Paper.** Cut the paper and card stock to a size which easily fit into the envelops.

3. **Collect Library Pockets.** Explore the public and school libraries in your area to see which ones are converting from a card system to a scan and computer operation. Ask the librarian to save all of the old pockets and cards. Pick them up at a convenient time.

4. **Collect Stickers.** Save all types of stickers which you receive free in the mail. For additional stickers, ask your parents to donate theirs.

5. Send for a Free WEE DELIVER Postal Kit. Send the request on your school's stationery. Your kit will include a:

♦ Sturdy cardboard mailbox

♦ Sturdy cardboard letter sort shelf

♦ Child-size mailbag

♦ Rubber stamps

♦ Video

♦ Teacher's guide

Send Your Request To:

WEE DELIVER PROGRAM
U.S. Postal Service
475 L'Enfant Plaza, SW Room 10541
Washington, DC 20260-3100

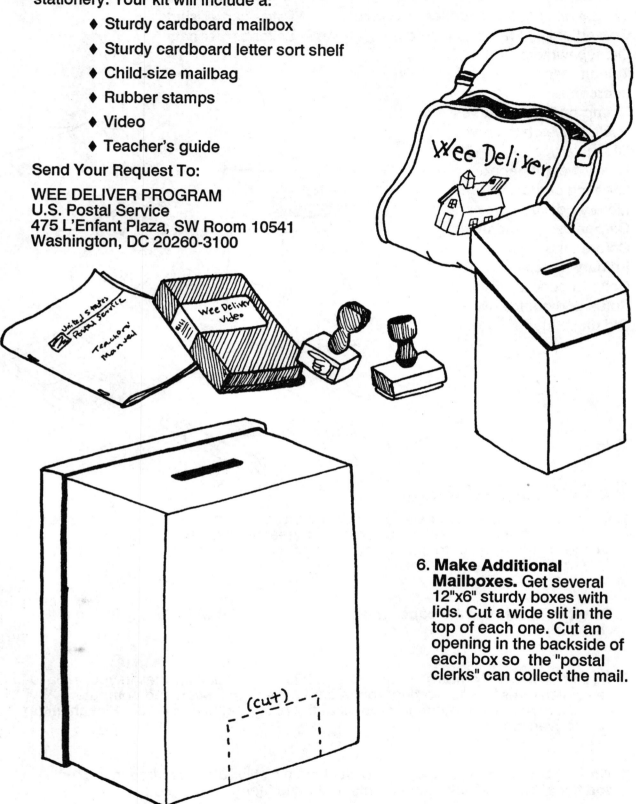

6. Make Additional Mailboxes. Get several 12"x6" sturdy boxes with lids. Cut a wide slit in the top of each one. Cut an opening in the backside of each box so the "postal clerks" can collect the mail.

(cut)

16

PLAY OPPORTUNITIES

At The Office is one of the younger children's favorite activities. It is soothing and immediately attracts their attention. They quickly become very busy using all the props. In addition it is easy to set up and can be used at a moment's notice.

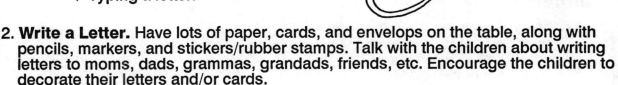

1. **Make a Call.** Use the telephone or intercom to "dial-up" a child. Talk about:
    - ♦ Who she's writing a letter to
    - ♦ Filling her mailbag with notes and cards
    - ♦ Sorting letters in the mail slots
    - ♦ Adding stamps to her letters
    - ♦ Typing a letter.

2. **Write a Letter.** Have lots of paper, cards, and envelops on the table, along with pencils, markers, and stickers/rubber stamps. Talk with the children about writing letters to moms, dads, grammas, grandads, friends, etc. Encourage the children to decorate their letters and/or cards.

3. **Mail a Letter.** Have mailboxes on the table. After children have written and sealed their letters, encourage them to mail the letters in the boxes.

4. **Collect the Mail.** After letters have been mailed, put a mailbag over your shoulder. Go to each box, and have the children get the mail and put it in your pouch. Deliver the mail to children playing in the room.

    VARIATIONS:
    - ♦ Let the children deliver the mail.
    - ♦ Let the children be letter carriers who carry and deliver the mail.

5. **Adult** "encourages" the play and encourages the children to use all the different props. She/he can:

   - ♦ Teach the children how to
       - Stuff the letters and cards into envelops
       - Lick the envelops closed
       - Put stamps and stickers on mail
       - Write on the carbonless paper.
   - ♦ Keep the props on the table
   - ♦ Empty filled mailbags and brief cases which the children have carried away from the office and left in other areas of the room
   - ♦ Help the children "write" letters, notes, cards, etc.
   - ♦ Be a letter carrier.

17

BABY

SET UP

Place

Baby is a very natural extension of the housekeeping area.

Setting*

1. To the existing housekeeping area add:
   - ♦ Several high chairs around the table
   - ♦ Cribs in a quiet area
   - ♦ Lots of baby dolls
   - ♦ Several bounce chairs

* If you provide infant care at your facility, trade or borrow a few things from the infant rooms, while your children are playing "baby."

18

PROPS

High chairs
Infant seats
Cribs
Bounce chairs
Rocking chairs
Baby toys
♦ Busy boxes
♦ Rattles
♦ Squeaker toys
♦ Music boxes
♦ Wind-up toys
Receiving blankets
Unbreakable bottles
Empty baby cereal boxes
Dishes
Silverware
Diaper bags
Empty powder containers
Changing pads
Several strollers and/or buggies
Baby hair brushes
Wash cloths
Towels
Infant front packs/backpacks

CLOTHES

Cloth/disposable diapers - Use
    masking or adhesive tape to fasten
    the diapers, or use disposable
    diapers with Velcro® closures
Bibs
Pre-mature baby clothes of all types
Sleepers with different fasteners:
♦ Snaps
♦ Zippers
♦ Velcro®
♦ Buttons

PREPARATION

None

19

PLAY OPPORTUNITIES

Babies is one of younger children's favorite activities. Take advantage of this natural enthusiasm and excitement, by playing "babies" often.

- ♦ If one of the teachers is expecting a baby

- ♦ When one of the children has a new brother or sister

- ♦ When a child is excited about something his baby sister/brother has just learned, such as how to play with a new toy.

1. **Undress and Dress Your Baby.** Young children especially like to undress the babies, so begin with dressed babies. After children have undressed the babies, encourage the children to put the clothes back on their babies, so they don't get cold.

   HINT: Help the children if they have difficulty putting the sleeves in the arm holes or legs in the pants. Talk about doing it gently so the babies do not get hurt.

2. **Feed Your Baby.** Put additional high chairs in the area. Have bibs, empty food containers, baby dishes and silverware, and baby bottles. Encourage the children to sit their babies in the high chairs or hold them in their arms. After feeding, remind the children to put a cloth over their shoulders and "burp" their babies.

   EXTENSION: Let the children sample different types of baby foods for a "taste-testing" snack.

3. **Change Your Baby's Diapers.** Set diaper pads, baby wipes, empty powder containers, and diapers on one of the shelves in the housekeeping area. Show the children how to lay their babies on the diaper pads, wipe them clean, and then put on diapers using tape to fasten them closed.

4. **Rock Your Baby.** Have several rocking chairs in the area, plus a music box on a nearby shelf. Let the children rock their babies. While rocking they could:

- ♦ Just be quiet because the baby is sleeping

- ♦ Talk softly to their babies

- ♦ Sing to their babies.

Rock-a-bye Baby
(adapted slightly)

Rock-a-bye baby
On the treetop
When the wind blows
The cradle with rock.

If the bough breaks
The cradle will fall
And I will catch baby
Cradle and all.

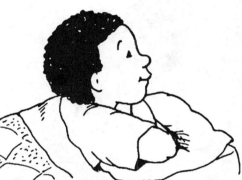

5. **Wrap Your Baby in a Blanket.** Have lots of babies and receiving blankets. Show the children how to lay the blankets on the table and wrap up the babies so they are warm and secure.

    HINT: The children like you to wrap the babies and then they can unwrap them. Help them learn to do both.

6. **Take Your Baby for a Walk.** If it is nice weather, take the babies, strollers, buggies, back and front packs, and blankets outside.

- ♦ Push the babies around the play area

- ♦ Swing babies while carrying them in the front packs

- ♦ Walk around the play area with babies in the back or front packs

- ♦ Lay several babies in a wagon and pull them around with a friend.

7. Play with Your Baby. Encourage the children to:
- ♦ Point to different body parts and name them
- ♦ Wind-up a music box and put it near the babies
- ♦ Sing chants and do the actions with their babies.

This Little Piggy

This little piggy went to market.
This little piggy stayed home.
This little piggy had roast beef.
This little piggy had none.
This little piggy, cried "*Wee, wee, wee, wee*"
All the way home.

Pat-a-cake

Pat-a-cake, pat-a cake
Baker's man.
Bake me a cake
As fast as you can.

Roll it, pat it
Mark it with a B.
Put it in the oven
For Baby and me.

Gitty-up
(Bounce baby gently on lap.)

Gitty-up, gitty-up, gitty-up
Up -- up!

Gitty-up, gitty-up, gitty-up
Up -- up!

Gitty-up, gitty-up, gitty-up
Up -- up!

Whooooooa ---------- Horsey!

8. Look at Baby Pictures. Display baby pictures at the children's eye level in different areas of your room. Talk with the children about what the babies are doing.
- ♦ Let children bring in photos of themselves as babies.
- ♦ Ask teachers to bring in photo albums of when they were babies.
- ♦ Put books about babies on the book shelf. (See BOOK LIST.)

EXTENSION: Put several empty cameras in the housekeeping area for children to take pictures/movies of their babies.

9. Visit from a Baby. Encourage your families to bring new babies to school for the children to see. Encourage the parent/s to stay for as long as they are comfortable. While there the parent could:
- ♦ Rock her baby
- ♦ Feed him
- ♦ Take him for a ride in a stroller
- ♦ Hold him so the children could see and talk to him
- ♦ Play with him.

10. **Play with Baby Toys.** Have a large container filled with lots of different rattles, wind-up toys, busy boxes, shakers, etc. Put the container on a large table and let the children play with toys they used to enjoy when they were babies.

11. **Bathe Your Baby.** Put a little warm water and baby soap bubbles in your water table. Set towels, empty powder containers, and receiving blankets on a nearby table. Let the children give the babies baths, dry them, and wrap them up so they do not catch colds.

12. **Put Your Baby to Bed.** Have sleepers and several cribs in the housekeeping area. Let the children get their babies ready for bed. They may want to sing their babies a song or "read" them a book before hugging them good night.

13. **Adult** "encourages" the play and helps the children gently and safely take care of, talk to, and play with their babies. She/he can:

♦ Sing songs

♦ Dress the babies

♦ Wrap the babies

♦ Help change the babies

♦ Join other "parents" who are taking their babies for a walk

♦ Talk about baby pictures

♦ Encourage families to bring in their babies for the children to see.

CAMPING

Place

In an open area of the room, plus housekeeping, water table, and outside.

Setting

1. Set up a small tent in the open area of your room. If you have access to a real tent, such as a pop-up, use it. If not, put a blanket over your climber or a sheet over a small table.

2. Build a campfire near the tent. Roll up sheets of newspaper into long and short tubes or use different length cardboard tubes. Build the campfire with the "logs."

3. Put several backpacks and picnic supplies in the housekeeping area.

4. Put construction paper fish in the water table and fishing poles nearby.

24

PROPS

"Toy" grill
Barbecue set
Pots/pans
Large spoons
Sleeping bags
Flashlights
Several fold-up maps
Compass
Coffee pot
Picnic supplies
Tin cups
Marshmallows

CLOTHES

Bandannas for the children's heads
Hiking boots
Sunglasses
Sun visors
Fishing hats
Bug catcher hats

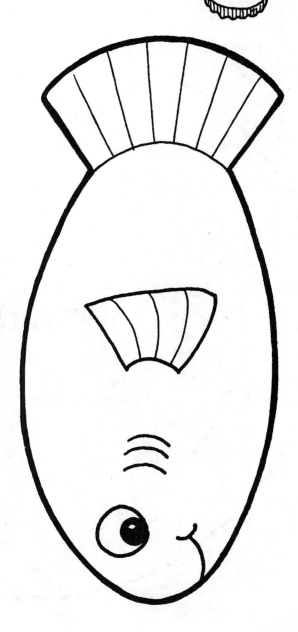

PREPARATION

1. Make The Fish And Fishing Poles

Fish

You'll Need
Construction paper
Metal paper clips

Make: Use the fish pattern and cut out 10 or more different colored fish. Put several paper clips on each one. (This will make it easier for the children to catch them.)

Fishing Poles

You'll Need
Dowel rods
Yarn
Small magnets

Make: Cut the dowel rods into 6" lengths. Cut the yarn into 12" lengths. Tie each piece of yarn to a dowel rod. Tie a small magnet to the other end of each piece of yarn.

2. Tie The Bandannas

Gather all the scarves, and tie them so that they will easily fit on the children's heads.

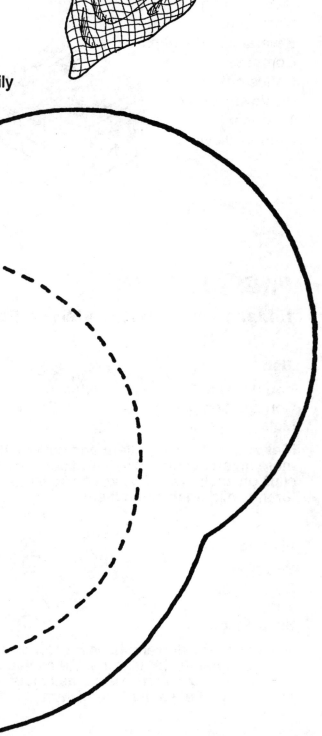

3. Make Visors

You'll Need
Posterboard

Make: Enlarge the pattern so that it fits easily on your children's heads. Make as many visors as you need.

(cut out)

PLAY OPPORTUNITIES

1. In the Tent.

♦ Put several sleeping bags in the tent. Let the children crawl inside the sleeping bags and "sleep." Every once in awhile peek inside and in a whisper voice encourage them to rest and be quiet. Some children may actually fall asleep.

♦ Have several of the children's favorite stories nearby. (See the book list for camping.) Let the children sit inside and outside the tent while you read and/or tell stories.

2. At the Campfire.

♦ The children may want to wear the bug hats and bandannas. Bring out the pots, pans, several spoons, and other cooking equipment you may have. Talk about what the children could cook, and then let them "cook" it over the fire.

♦ Have sticks and let the children "cook" hot dogs.

♦ Instead of a fire, bring out a grill and barbecue tools. Let the children "cook" over this type of fire.

♦ Have the plates and tin cups. Sit around the fire and "eat" the food you prepared.

♦ Sing the children's favorite songs while sitting around the campfire. You could sing:

Bear Went Over the Mountain

Row, Row, Row Your Boat

Ring Around the Rosie

Happy Birthday

Twinkle, Twinkle Little Star

Hokey Pokey

Wheels On the Bus

Old McDonald

Are You Sleeping
(Use children's names.)

3. **Have a Picnic.** The children may want to wear the sun visors, hats, and sunglasses. Put the picnic supplies and a blanket in several of the backpacks. Let the children carry them as they "hike" around the room to the picnic area. Unfold the blanket, sit around it, and have your picnic.

4. **Go Fishing.** Let the children put on fishing hats and go fishing in the water table. As the children catch the fish, talk with them about how they caught their fish, the color of their fish, and so on. Have a "fishing bucket" near the fishing hole. As the children catch fish, put them in the bucket. When it's full, put the fish back in the water.

5. **Go Hunting.** Turn off the lights in the classroom. Give the children flashlights and go for a hike. What do you see? (The children love this activity. Have as many flashlights as possible. It is great to have one for each child.)

6. **Outside Camping.** Camping easily lends itself to inside and outside play. Because you have more space, use a larger tent and get several more sleeping bags. All of the above activities can easily be done outside. In addition you can:

   ♦ Have real marshmallows on the sticks and let the children "roast" them over the "fire" and enjoy them for a little treat.

   ♦ Get the compass, and go for a "hike" around the play area. Look at the bugs, birds, and trees. Take time to let the children see how the compass moves as you turn in different directions. HAPPY HIKING!

   ♦ Pour water in a large plastic container such as your water table or a small pool. Let the children put on their smocks and wash the camping dishes and pans.

CONSTRUCTION

Place

In the block area or adjacent to it.

Setting

1. Incorporate a table or work bench along one side of the block area. If there is not enough room in the block center, put the table at the end of one shelf in the area.

2. Build a road using masking tape. Start it at the block area, wind it through part of the classroom, and then come back to the block area.

3. Have the props readily available. You will be rotating these as the children want to play with or "fix" them.

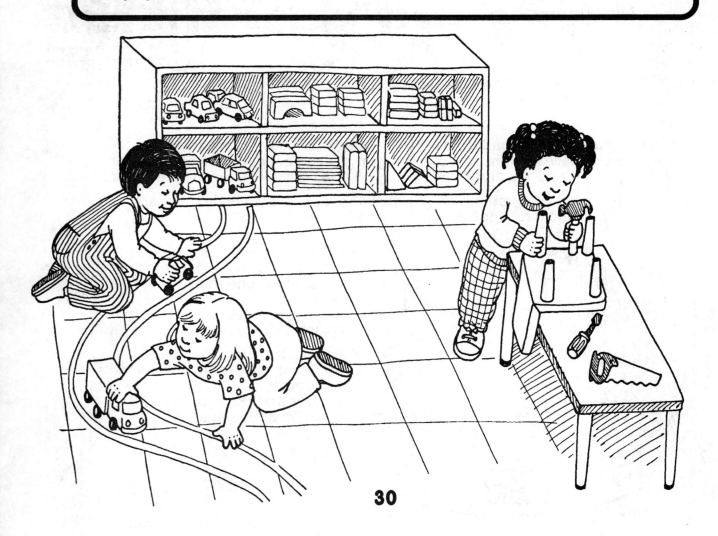

30

PROPS

Plastic tools
Tool bench
Pounding bench
Pounding peg bench
Lunch boxes
Toy garages
Toy parking lots
Small cars and trucks
Riding toys
Chairs

CLOTHES

Safety goggles
Tool belts
Carpenter aprons
Construction hats
Construction boots
  (Remember Safety: Be sure that the laces are pre-tied and/or short enough so that children cannot trip on them.)

Flannel shirts

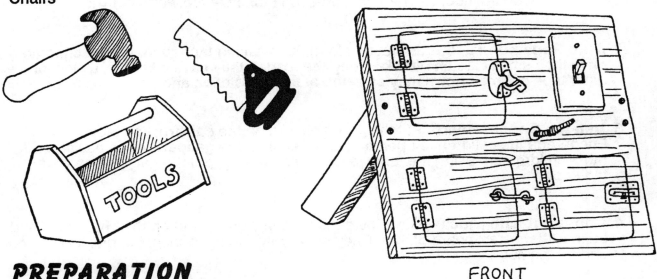

FRONT

PREPARATION

1. Make A Gadget Board

You'll Need

Piece of 2'x3' plywood
Different easy gadgets
♦ Latch
♦ Light switch
♦ Door stopper which goes "bing" when you work it
♦ Outdoor water faucet
♦ Inside water faucet

To Make

1) Sand the plywood so it is smooth and safe.

2) Paint it with a non-toxic paint.

3) Securely attach all of the "gadgets."

PLAY OPPORTUNITIES

1. **At the Repair Shop.** The "repair shop" suggests many types of "fixing" activities. For example:

   ♦ The children's favorite thing to "repair" is their classroom chairs. They like to turn them upside down on the repair table and then use their tools to tighten the screws, and fix the legs and seats. After the chairs are fixed, have the children put them back in the classroom.

   ♦ Let the children "drive" their cars, trucks, and other riding vehicles to the repair shop and fix them.

   ♦ Bring a very small table into the repair shop. Turn it upside down and set it on the floor near the construction table. Let the workers fix it.

2. **Auto Repair.** Put a toy gas station along the masking tape road. Let the children drive their small cars and trucks along the road. If they have a flat tire, a stall, or other type of break-down they can stop at the gas station and get it repaired.

3. **Use the Gadget Board.** Put the gadget board on the construction table. Encourage the children to open and close each of the gadgets. If it is easier, or if other children are using the table to repair something, put the gadget board on the floor.

4. **Construct with Blocks.** Have the construction workers put on their hard hats and build with the cardboard blocks. They especially like to connect the blocks end-to end on the floor.

5. Pound-Pound.

♦ Put the pounding bench and/or peg bench on the construction table. Let the construction workers use their hammers and pound the "nails."

♦ Get a giant piece of styrofoam and lots of golf tees and hammers. Let the workers hold the "nails" and carefully pound them into the styrofoam.

♦ Stick 4-6 large colored dots on the construction table. Let the workers pound the dots with their hammers.

HINT: This is an especially good activity for children who are using hammers for the first time.

6. Eat Lunch.
Lunchtime at the construction site! Have all the workers carry their lunch boxes to the eating area, sit down, and eat together.

7. Adult "encourages" the play. She/he can:

♦ Help move furniture in and out of the repair shop

♦ Tie carpenter aprons for the workers

♦ Direct traffic along the masking tape road

♦ Help drivers who have gotten stuck along the highway

♦ Talk with the children as they play with the gadgets on the gadget board

♦ Help the builders lay the "bricks" along the floor

♦ Eat lunch with the construction workers

DOCTOR

Place

In the block area or other large space.

Setting

1. Put several cots next to each other. Cover each one with a twin-size white bedsheet. (The fitted type work best.)

2. Tack a "height chart" to the wall in the area.

3. Put a scale on the floor near the height chart. Hang a "weight chart" near the scale.

4. Set a baby scale on a shelf.

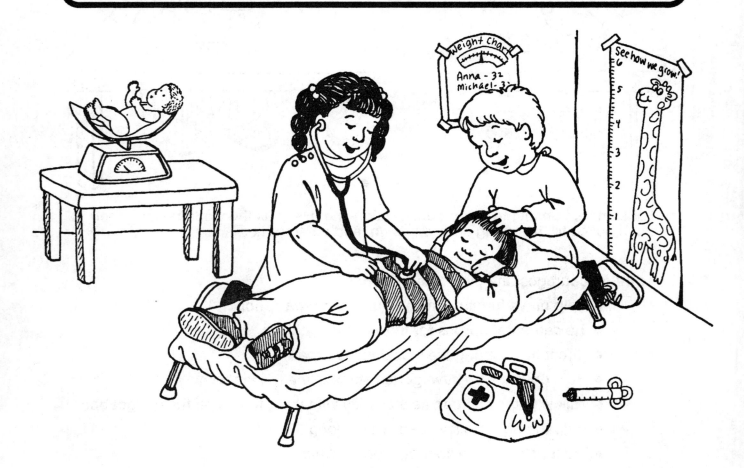

PROPS

Several doctor's bags with play accessories:
♦ Stethoscopes
♦ Ear lights
♦ Ace bandages
♦ Blood pressure gauges
♦ Syringes

Metal bandage boxes

Baby dolls

Stuffed animals

Posters

Medical equipment, such as child-size:
♦ Wheel chairs
♦ Braces
♦ Crutches
♦ Walkers
♦ Canes

CLOTHES

Hospital gowns including head and foot gear
(Could use lightweight shower caps for head gear.)

Laboratory coats or white shirts

Latex gloves

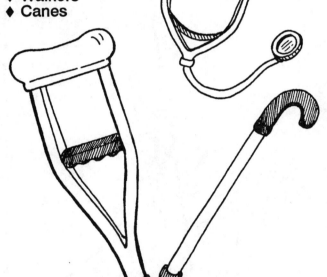

PREPARATION

1. Get Hospital Clothes

♦ Call the public relations office for the pediatric department of your local hospital or medical center. Tell the office worker about your classroom and ask if they would donate hospital gowns for the children to use.

♦ Ask parents who are associated with the medical profession to donate appropriate clothes.

2. Make A Height Chart

Cut a piece of butcher paper six to eight feet long. Along the left side mark off the inches and feet. Draw the outline of a giraffe next to the measurements.

3. Make A Weight Chart

Cut a giant scale from a piece of posterboard.

4. Get Posters

Good sources for posters are:
Your local physician, hospital, and/or pharmacy
Pharmaceutical companies
Medical laboratories
Medical organizations

Look for posters which portray:
Eye charts
Height and weight information
Children's bodies
Skeletal systems
Doctors and nurses

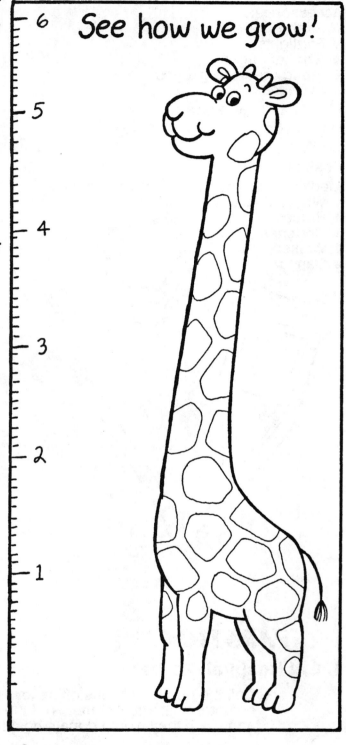

See how we grow!

PLAY OPPORTUNITIES

1. **Children's Heights.** Have each child stand in front of the giraffe pictured on the height chart. Use a dark pen and mark his/her height on the giraffe with a dash and then write his/her name next to the dash.

   HINT: This is a great activity to do several times a year, so the children understand that they are getting taller. Use a different color marker each time.

2. **Children's Weights.** Have each child stand on the scale. Read the child's weight to him/her and then record it on the giant posterboard scale.

   HINT: This is a great activity to do several times a year, so that the children can see that they are gaining weight -- getting bigger.

3. **Going to the Hospital.** Set up the hospital when a child or adult in the classroom is going to the hospital for several days or more. This is a good time to add several pieces of equipment for disabilities. As the children are playing, talk about the person who is going to the hospital, why she/he is going, and when she/he will return to school. Keep the hospital set up while the person is away.

EXTENSION: Make a giant mural for him/her and send it so she/he can hang it on the hospital wall or door.

4. **Doctor's Appointment.** Children can put on the doctor's clothes and be doctors. They can:

- ♦ Check ears
- ♦ Give shoots
- ♦ Measure heights and weights
- ♦ Listen to hearts
- ♦ Put on bandages
- ♦ Examine babies and stuffed animals
- ♦ Wrap gauze bandages.

5. **Fill the Doctor Bag.** Put the doctor's equipment and bags on the shelf in the doctor's area. Let the children fill and empty the bags as they choose.

6. **Adult** "encourages" the play by being the patient, doctor, or parent bringing a child to the doctor.

When the patient, she/he can:

- ♦ Tell the doctor what hurts
- ♦ Let the doctor "fix" her/him
- ♦ Get a shot
- ♦ Have her/his ears checked
- ♦ Etc.

When the doctor, she/he can:

- ♦ Listen to the patients
- ♦ "Fix" the children who are sick
- ♦ Weigh and measure the children
- ♦ Feel the children's arms and legs to see if they are healthy
- ♦ Talk about going to the hospital
- ♦ Wrap bandages on children and stuffed animals who got cut.

When the parent, she/he can:

- ♦ Take the child to the doctor
- ♦ Tell the doctor what is wrong with the child
- ♦ Hold the child or stuffed animal on her/his lap while the doctor examines the child who is sick.

FIREFIGHTERS

SET UP

Place

In the area you have your climber. The climber will be the focal point of the firefighting activity, so you will also need to have space around it.

Setting

1. The climber becomes the "house" which catches fire.

2. Have several riding toys for fire engines. Put these near the climber. If you do not have riding toys, use large, sturdy cardboard boxes for fire trucks. Each box should be large enough for several children, plus their fire equipment.

3. Have one riding toy be the ambulance. If you do not have one, use a large, sturdy cardboard box.

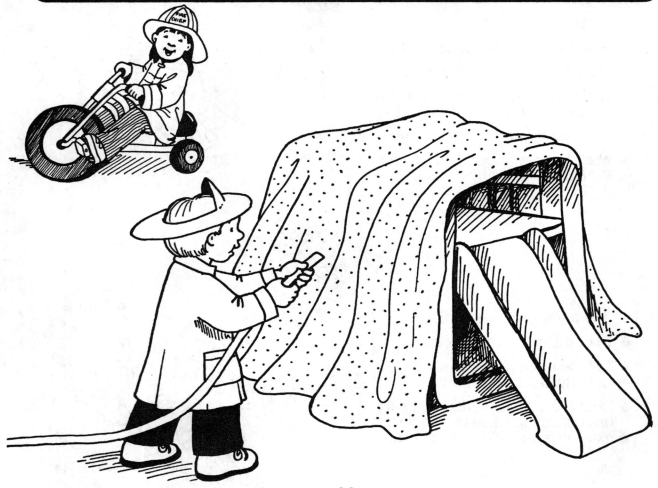

PROPS

Old vacuum cleaner hose
Piece of old garden hose
First aid box

CLOTHES

Several rubber raincoats or slickers
Several pairs of rubber boots
Fire hats/headbands
Firefighter badges

PREPARATION

1. Make Firefighter Headbands

You'll Need
11"x14" red, black, and yellow poster-board/construction paper

Make: For each headband, cut a piece of paper into a large oval. Cut a partial oval out of the middle of the large oval, leaving the front side attached. Flip-up the inside oval, exposing the opening for the child to put on her head. (See illustration.)

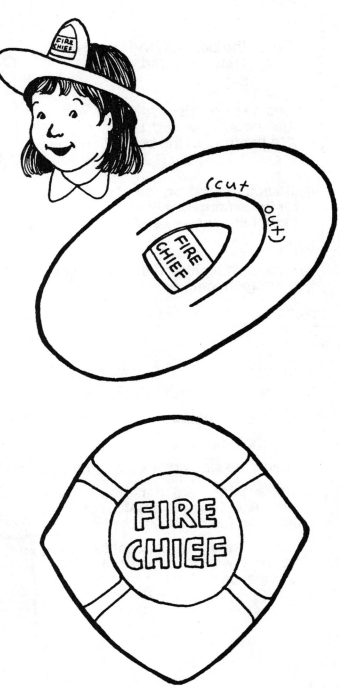

2. Make Firefighter Badges

You'll Need
Construction paper
Yarn or tape

Make: Duplicate the pattern on construction paper as many times as you need. Cut out the badges. Punch a hole in the top of each badge and loop a piece of yarn through it. Let the children wear the badges around their necks. If you prefer, put a loop of tape on the back of each badge and have the children stick the badges to their shirts.

3. Pack The First Aid Kit

Get gauze, bandages, cotton balls, stethoscope etc. and put them in the first aid kit.

4. Make The Fire Trucks

To make each fire truck:

1) Cut the box down so that the sides are about 12" high -- low enough for the "firefighters" to get in and out, but high enough to feel like a fire truck.

2) Cover the box with red fabric or spray paint it with red paint.

3) Use a sturdy disposable plate for the "steering wheel." Loosely attach it to the front of the box with a brad.

4) Stick a red ball on top of a yardstick for the emergency light. Glue it in one of the corners of the box.

5) Draw headlights on the front with permanent marker.

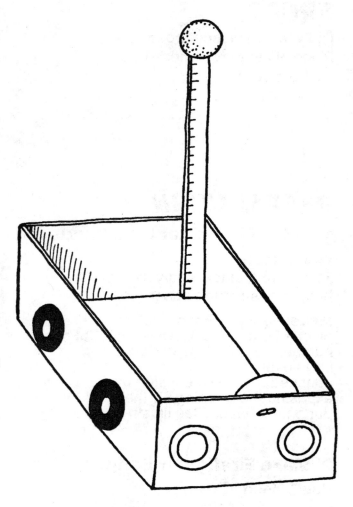

5. Make The Ambulances

To make the ambulance:

1) Cut the box down so that it is easy for children to get in and out.

2) Cover the sides of the box with white paint, fabric, or adhesive paper.

3) Use a permanent marker to draw a large Red Cross symbol on each side and headlights in the front.

4) Loosely attach a disposable plate "steering wheel" to the front of the ambulance with a brad.

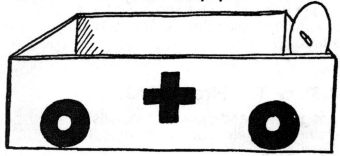

42

PLAY OPPORTUNITIES

1. **Put Out the Fire.** Have someone shout out that the house has caught on fire. Call for the firefighters. Have them get dressed, come to the fire, and put it out.

   ♦ The firefighters can drag their hoses and spray the fire until it is out.

   ♦ The firefighters can drag their hoses as they climb up the climber. When they get up high they can spray the fire with lots of water.

   ♦ Everyone can sing the firefighting song while putting out the fire.

   LET'S BE FIREFIGHTERS
   (tune: 1 Little, 2 Little, 3 Little Children)
   Hurry, hurry drive the fire truck.
   Hurry, hurry drive the fire truck.
   Hurry, hurry drive the fire truck.
   On a sunny morning.
   (Drive.)

   Hurry, hurry turn the corner...
   (Tip to one side.)
   Hurry, hurry find the fire...
   (Look around.)
   Hurry, hurry drag the hoses...
   (Pull the hoses.)
   Hurry, hurry spray the water...
   (Spray hoses.)
   Hurry, hurry back to the station...
   (Drive.)

2. **Firefighting Sounds.**

   ♦ As the children are driving their fire trucks to the fire, they can make the siren and horn-honking noises.

   ♦ As the children are spraying the fire with water, they can make the spraying sounds.

3. **Get the Paramedics.** Have some of the children drive the ambulance to the fire and help people who have gotten hurt. Lay them down and test their hearts. Fix them up if they need bandages, etc.

4. **Adult** "encourages" the play and helps the children be firefighters who are trying to put out the fire. She/he can:

   ♦ Help the children find the fire by pointing to it and calling out, "*Oh look, the house is on fire! Spray water over there.*"

GROCERY STORE

SET UP

Place

In the block area or any other open space in the classroom.

Setting

1. Set an empty shelf along one side of your block area. If you do not have an available shelf, stack your hollow blocks into a shelf. You might stack them 5 blocks long and 4 high.

2. Put the food boxes, cartons, bottles, and cans on the grocery shelf.

3. Place a table near the grocery shelves for the check-out counter. Put the grocery bags, cash registers, and/or calculators on the table.

4. Have grocery carts and baskets nearby.

PROPS

Cash registers
Play money
Lots of plastic foods such as:
♦ Fruit
♦ Vegetables
♦ Breads
♦ Meats
♦ Eggs
♦ Etc.
Lots of sturdy food containers:
♦ Plastic bottles
♦ Egg cartons
♦ Large cardboard boxes
♦ Cans with rounded edges (safety)
Grocery baskets
Toy grocery carts
Dolls
Wagon
Calculators
Banners
Posters

CLOTHES

White construction hats
White lab coats
Grocery smocks
Aprons
Wallets
Purses

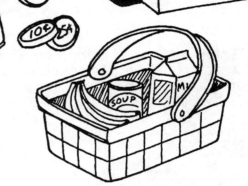

PREPARATION

1. Collect Product Aprons

In many grocery stores, different manufacturers have representatives who give samples of their products to the shoppers. These representatives usually wear aprons with the product name and logo. Ask the representatives if they would be willing to donate their aprons to your classroom after they get new ones.

2. Get Posters And Banners

Good sources for posters/banners are:
Your local grocery store
Food manufacturers
Delivery personnel
Nutrition council
Milk association

Look for posters/banners which portray:
Food groups
Variety of foods such as breads
Grocery store workers
Pricing information

3. Make Paper Plate Steering Wheels

Get several sturdy paper plates. Cut a kidney-shaped hole for the children's hands to fit into, on two sides of each plate. Reinforce the two holes with tape.

PLAY OPPORTUNITIES

1. **Drive to the Grocery Store.** Have the children get their wallets and purses and drive to the grocery store. If they are going to take their babies, remind the "moms and dads" to put their babies in car seats and buckle them up.

2. **Go Shopping.** Have the shoppers get grocery carts or baskets as they enter the store. Let them:

    ♦ Fill up their carts/baskets with groceries

    ♦ Push the carts around

    ♦ Talk to store workers

    ♦ Visit with friends who are shopping

    ♦ Etc.

3. **Take the Babies Shopping.** Encourage the children to get their purses and wallets, gently put their babies in the wagons and walk to the grocery store. They may want to put car seats in the wagons for the babies to sit in, and/or wrap their babies in blankets.

4. Check Out the Groceries. Have at least one cash register and several calculators on the "check out" table. The children can:

- ◆ Put their groceries on the table
- ◆ Work the cash register and calculators
- ◆ Pay for the groceries
- ◆ Bag the groceries
- ◆ Put the groceries in the wagon and carry them home.

5. Adult "encourages" the play and helps the children get involved with shopping as she/he:

- ◆ Checks out the groceries
- ◆ Re-stocks the grocery shelves
- ◆ Shops for groceries
- ◆ Bags the groceries
- ◆ Talks with the children about the food they are buying.

HAIR STYLIST

— SET UP —

Place

Large table near the housekeeping area.

Setting

1. Lay your unbreakable full-length mirror on its side, in the middle of a large table. (Could also use a large, unbreakable tri-fold mirror.)

2. Put chairs around the entire table.

3. Set the "hair" props on the table in front of the mirror.*

4. Set the "beauty" and "shaving" props on the table in back of the mirror.

5. If you have another full-length mirror stand it near the table.

   *Hair props and equipment must be used once and then sanitized.

HAIR PROPS

Plastic combs
Straightening combs
Plastic brushes
Posterboard scissors
Wigs on manikins
Unbreakable hand mirrors
Little water in hair spray bottles
Hand held hair dryers (cut cords)
Empty shampoo bottles
Empty ultra sheen balm containers
Decorative hair combs
Barrettes
Hair extensions
Scrunches
Hair clips
Sponge rollers
Velcro® rollers
Mesh rollers
Ponytail holders
Curling irons (cut cords)
Ribbons
Headbands

CLOTHES

Plastic capes
Costume jewelry
Purses
Shower caps
Silky caps
Towels

BEAUTY PROPS

Fingernail brushes
Empty, unbreakable nail polish bottles
Nail files with rounded ends
Empty bath powder puff containers
Empty unbreakable perfume
    containers
"Toy" nail sets

SHAVING PROPS

Shaving cream
Popsicle sticks
Paper towels

PREPARATION

1. Make Cardboard Scissors

You'll Need
Posterboard
Pair of children's rounded scissors

Make

Trace each side of an opened pair of scissors on posterboard/cardboard. Cut out each side and then attach them with a brad so the "scissors" open and close. Repeat the process to make lots of scissors.

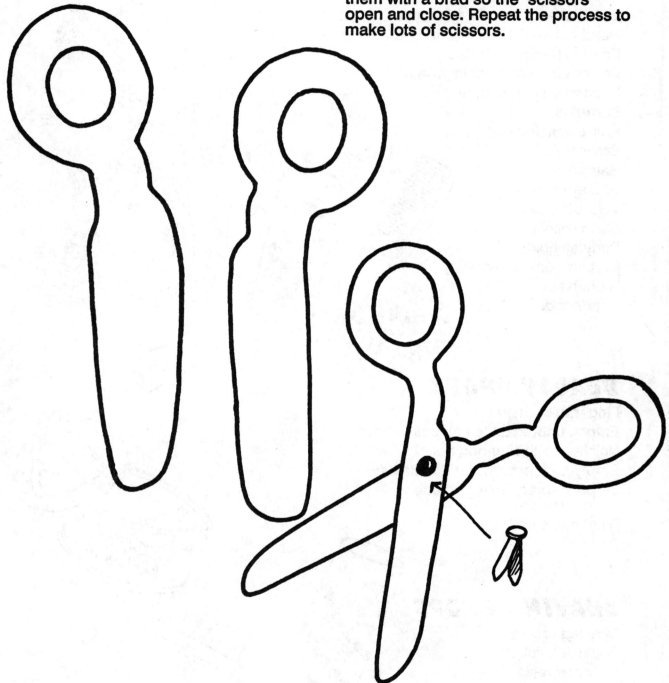

PLAY OPPORTUNITIES

1. **Get a Hair Cut.** Put several plastic capes, combs, pairs of posterboard scissors, and a variety of hair decorations on the table. Let the children use the scissors to "cut" each other's hair. Encourage the children to:

- ♦ Watch themselves get haircuts in the mirror
- ♦ Comb their hair
- ♦ Decorate their hair with ribbons, barrettes, headbands, etc.

HINT: Combing a child's hair is usually very soothing to her/him. When a child needs to calm down, take out a few props and begin to do the child's hair.

2. **Get a Shampoo.** Put shampoo bottles, towels, plastic rollers, and curling irons on the table. Shampooing suggests many types of play:

- ♦ Washing hair
- ♦ Drying hair with a hair dryer
- ♦ Rolling hair in rollers
- ♦ Curling hair with a curling iron
- ♦ Straightening hair
- ♦ Adding hair decorations
- ♦ Adding more grease.

HINT: Children love to shampoo and "fix" adult's hair. Encourage them to use different hair decorations, hair styles, etc.

3. **"Fix" the Wigs.** Set several manikins on the table with different wigs. Have a variety of hair props. Let the children:

- ♦ Cut the wigs
- ♦ Shampoo the wigs
- ♦ Add hair decorations
- ♦ Curl the wigs
- ♦ Add hair extensions

4. **Get a Shave.** Have shaving cream and popsicle sticks in a small basket on the table. Let the children put on shaving capes, "lather up" with shaving cream, and then use the popsicle sticks to give themselves and/or each other shaves.

5. **Do Your Nails.** Set the nail files, fingernail brushes, and empty polish containers on the table. Let the children:

- ♦ File each other's nails
- ♦ Massage each other's hands and fingers with lotion
- ♦ Polish each other's nails.

6. **Moisturize Your Skin.** Have several bottles of hand lotion. Squirt some lotion onto a child's hand. Let him rub it on his hands and fingers, up and down his arms, and on his cheeks.

7. **Put on Jewelry.** Put several hand held mirrors on the table, plus all of your larger mirrors. Have a box of beads, necklaces, bracelets, earrings, belts, etc. Set it on the table. Let the children dress up.

8. **Adult** "encourages" the play by being aware of when the children need help. Children like to do these activities and can do many of them by themselves, but sometimes need help and encouragement. Adults can:

   ♦ Get their hair cut and shampooed

   ♦ Polish the children's nails

   ♦ Fasten the plastic capes

   ♦ Massage children's hands and fingers.

   ♦ Help attach hair decorations.

HAPPY BIRTHDAY

SET UP

Place

In the housekeeping area.

Setting

1. Set the table with a birthday tablecloth, plates, and napkins.

2. Have birthday hats and favors by each plate.

3. Put the birthday presents in a big basket.

4. Hang dress up clothes on a clothes pole. Stand the full length mirror near the clothes.

5. Drape colorful streamers from the ceiling.

PROPS*

Lots of invitations
Empty gift boxes/lids
Favors -- shakers, rattlers
Tablecloths
Bags
Streamers
Banners
Plates
Napkins
Birthday cake
Candles
Full length mirror
* Ask your families to donate their extra birthday favors, bags, invitations, and table settings.

CLOTHES

Purses
Birthday hats
Party dress ups
♦ Fancy shoes
♦ Blazers
♦ Vests
♦ Gloves
♦ Button down shirts
♦ Ties

PREPARATION

1. Wrap Gifts

You'll Need
Sturdy gift boxes/lids
Birthday wrapping paper

Wrap the Boxes

Wrap the top and bottom of each gift box separately so that the top simply lifts off.

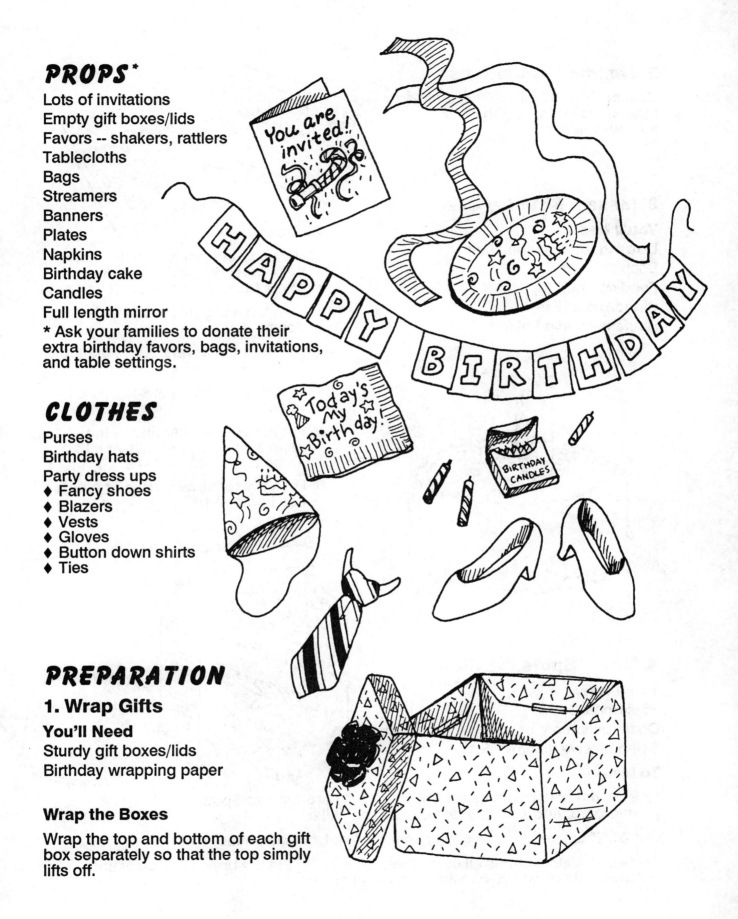

2. Laminate Invitations

Collect all your invitations. Laminate them or cover them with clear adhesive paper.

3. Make a Birthday Cake

You'll Need
Large margarine container
Soap powder
Food coloring (optional)
Birthday candles
Birthday candle holders

To Make:

1) Mix soap powder and water into a thick "frosting." (Add food coloring to the frosting if you want it colored.)

2) Turn the margarine tub upside down.

3) Carefully cut several X's in the top of the cake.

4) Frost the tub with the soap powder frosting.

5) Put the birthday candles in the candle holders. Insert them into the Xs on the top of the cake.

6) Let it dry for several days or until it has hardened.

4. Make "Spots the Clown"

You'll Need
Posterboard
Construction paper
Self-adhesive Velcro® dots

To Make:

Enlarge the pattern on the next page, and draw a full-size Spots the Clown on posterboard. Add as many features as you'd like.

Cut 20, 2" colored construction paper circles. Laminate them.

Spread 20 Velcro® dots all over Spots clown suit. Put the opposite side of the Velcro® dots on the 20 construction paper circles.

SPOTS THE CLOWN

PLAY OPPORTUNITIES

1. **Happy Birthday.** Birthdays occur throughout the year. Each time a child or adult in your room is celebrating a birthday, bring out the birthday props and have a party. During the day the children can:

   ♦ Set the birthday table

   ♦ Decorate with banners and streamers

   ♦ Sing "*Happy Birthday*"

   ♦ Dress up for the party

   ♦ Cut the birthday cake and eat it.

2. **Blow Out the Candles.** Have the birthday child carry the cake to the table. Sing "*Happy Birthday*" and then blow out the candles. Clap for the birthday children!! (YEAH) Sing "*Happy Birthday*" again and again.

   HINT: "*Happy Birthday*" is the children's favorite song. They will want to sing it over and over again.

3. **Open the Presents.** Let the children fill the birthday boxes with toys from around the room, and bring them to the party. After singing, pass out the gifts and let the children open them. Look at the gifts and clap for each one.

4. **Pass Out the Invitations.** Have lots of invitations available. Let the children put them in their purses, walk around the room, and pass them out to all the children. When a child gets one he should come to the party.

5. **Play Birthday Games.** After singing "*Happy Birthday*" several times, play simple games with all the children.

   - Bozo Buckets
   - Give "Spots the Clown" his colored circles
   - London Bridges Falling Down
   - Ring Around the Rosie

6. **Adult** "encourages" the birthday party play by:

   - Singing "*Happy Birthday*" with the children
   - Helping the children decorate
   - Playing games.

HOUSEKEEPING
DO BAKING AND COOKING

SET UP

Place

In the housekeeping area.

Setting

1. Have all the food ingredients in a basket or on a large tray. Set it on a shelf.

2. Bring the utensils, mixing bowls, and baking containers into the area. Set them on a shelf within easy reach.

3. Prepare the food on the kitchen table.

4. After making the real food with the children, put playdough and baking containers in housekeeping. Encourage the children to continue "baking and cooking."

PEANUT BUTTER
BALLS

Supplies and Materials
1 cup low-fat peanut butter
1 cup oatmeal
1/2 cup honey
1 cup non-fat powdered milk

Make the Balls
(Remember to wash hands before you begin.)

1. Let the children help you:
    ♦ Put the oatmeal and powdered milk in a large bowl and mix them together.
    ♦ Add the honey and peanut butter to the dry ingredients and mix them all together with a large wooden spoon.
    ♦ Continue to mix the dough until it forms one large ball.

2. Give each child a spoonful of the peanut butter mixture. Encourage him to form the dough into bite-size balls.

THUMB PRINT
COOKIES

Supplies and Materials
2 cups of flour
1t salt
2/3 cup oil
4-5T water

Make the Cookies
(Remember to wash hands before you begin.)

1. Let the children help you:
    ♦ Put the flour and salt in a large bowl and mix them together.
    ♦ Add the oil and water.
    ♦ Use a fork or hands to mix the ingredients together until they form a ball.
2. Have each child use a small spoon to scoop a little bit of cookie dough from the big ball, form it into a shape, and set it on a greased cookie sheet.
3. Have him make a thumb print in his cookie.
4. Bake the THUMB PRINT COOKIES at 325 degrees for 10 minutes.
5. Let them cool and then fill them with peanut butter or cream cheese.

HOUSEKEEPING
CARE FOR THE PETS

— SET UP —

Place

In the housekeeping area.

Setting

1. Put an animal bed and food bowl on the floor in an empty corner of the area.
2. Place several animals wearing leashes next to the table.
3. Set several empty animal food boxes on the kitchen shelf.
4. Tape pictures of pets on the cabinet doors.

PROPS

Animal bed
Pet brushes
Pet toys
Boxes of pet food
Lots of plastic/stuffed animals
Leashes for every pet
Posters and pictures

CLOTHES

Veterinarian lab coat.

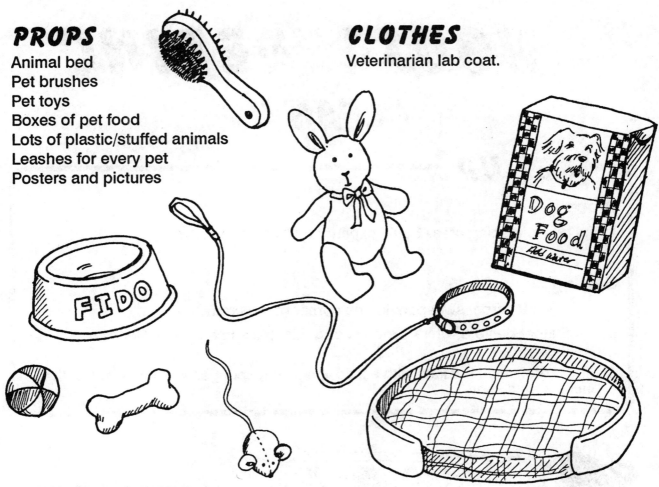

PREPARATION

1. Get Posters/Pictures

Good sources for posters/pictures are:
Pet clubs
Veterinary clinics
Pet magazines
Pet food companies

Look for posters/pictures which portray:
Different types of pets
Pets playing with toys
People playing with pets
Pets sleeping and eating

PLAY OPPORTUNITIES

1. **Adult** "encourages" the play and helps the children care for and play with their pets. She/he can:
   - Help children feed the pets
   - Talk with children while they walk their pets
   - Sit with children as they brush their pet's fur
   - Help children be gentle with their pets
   - Take pets to the veterinarian
   - Take the pets outside and walk them around the playground.

HOUSEKEEPING
CLEAN UP

SET UP

Place

In the housekeeping area. Could expand to all areas of the room.

Setting

1. Put several carpet sweepers in one corner of the area.

2. Put feather dusters, whisk brooms, and dust pans in a basket. Set it by a cabinet.

3. Fill several small buckets with a little water. Put sponges in each one. Set the buckets on a shelf.

PROPS

Carpet sweepers
Feather dusters
Whisk brooms
Dust pans
Small buckets with handles
Sponges
Dust cloths

CLOTHES

Aprons

PLAY OPPORTUNITIES

1. **Adult** "encourages" the play and helps the children clean up the housekeeping area. She/he can:

   ♦ Clean with the children

   ♦ Hold the dust pan while a child "brooms in" the dust

   ♦ Tie aprons for the "cleaning crew"

   ♦ Keep water in the small buckets

   ♦ Direct special outside "cleaning projects" such as

   - Bringing chairs outside and washing them

   - Scrubbing the outside riding toys

   - Washing the outside equipment and tables

   - Hosing off the sidewalks and/or other surfaces.

HOUSEKEEPING
DO THE LAUNDRY

Place

In the water table or other very large tub.

Inside Setting

1. Pour a little water in your water table. Add dish soap.

2. Have a drying rack next to the water table. Put heavy towels or large, shallow tubs under the rack to catch the dripping water. (Remember safety.)

Outside Setting

1. In a little travelled area of your playground, put several laundry tubs on the ground. Pour a little water in each one. Add dish soap.

2. Hang a clothesline at the children's reach. (Remember safety.) Have a bag of clothespins.

PROPS

Dish soap
Dish or laundry tubs
Clothesline
Clothespins
Drying rack
Heavy towels

CLOTHES

Doll clothes
Children's smocks

PLAY OPPORTUNITIES

1. **Adult** "encourages" the play and helps the children do the laundry. She/he can:

   ◆ Keep the tubs filled with a little water

   ◆ Help children hang clothes from the clothesline

   ◆ Show children how to use the clothespins

   ◆ Keep towels under wet clothes to absorb dripping water

   ◆ Wash clothes with the children

   ◆ Talk about washing and drying clothes at home or at the laundromat.

HOUSEKEEPING
GET DRESSED UP

SET UP

Place

In the housekeeping area.

Setting

1. Put the full length mirror near the dress up clothes.

2. Put hand mirrors on different shelves.

3. Hang fancy clothes on a clothes tree.

PROPS

Full length mirror
Several unbreakable hand mirrors
Clothes tree
Tri-fold mirror
Purses
Artificial bouquets of flowers

CLOTHES

Jewelry
Scarves
Ballet and dance outfits
Large variety of hats
Fancy dresses
Suit coats
Shoes
Ties

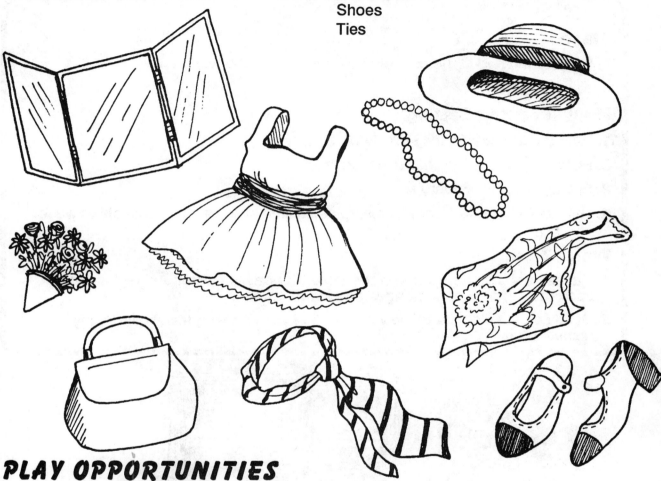

PLAY OPPORTUNITIES

1. **Adult** "encourages" the play and encourages children to dress up. She/he can:

   ♦ Talk with children about where they are going after they get dressed up

   ♦ Talk with children about the fancy clothes they are wearing

   ♦ Ask children to look at themselves in the mirror

   ♦ Help children put on the ballet and dance clothes over their regular clothes

   ♦ Set up a special hat party

   ♦ Get married to one of the children.

HOUSEKEEPING
WASH THE DISHES

— SET UP —

Place

In the sink located in the housekeeping area or in the water table.

Housekeeping Setting

1. Pour a little water in the sink. Add dish soap.

2. Put sponges and scrub brushes in the sink.

3. Set drying towels nearby.

4. Have unbreakable dishes, cups, pans, mixing spoons, etc. available to wash.

Water Table Setting

1. Put several dish tubs in the water table. Pour a little water and dish soap in each tub. Add several sponges and scrub brushes.

2. Set a small table next to the water table. Put the drying towels and "dirty dishes" on it.

70

PROPS

Lots of unbreakable dishes, pots,
    pans, and cooking utensils
Lots of sponges
Handy wipes
Scrub brushes
Several dish tubs
Dish soap
Drying towels

CLOTHES

Children's smocks

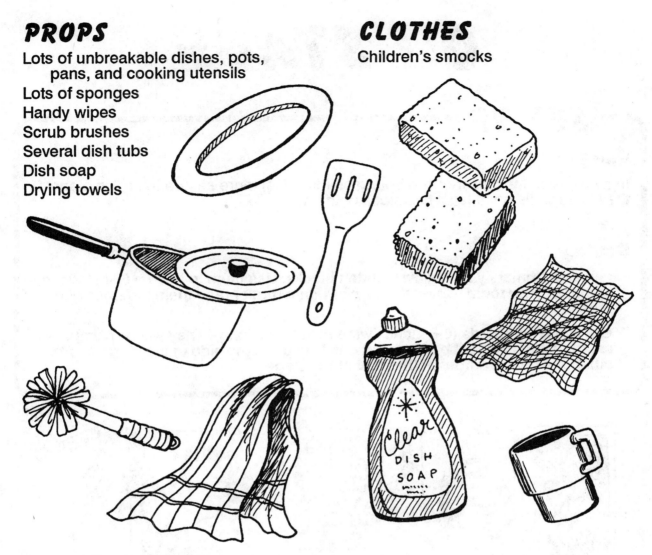

PREPARATION

1. Cut the sponges and handy wipes into small pieces. (The children need small pieces so the washing process does not become too cumbersome.)

PLAY OPPORTUNITIES

1. **Adult** "encourages" the play and helps the children wash and dry the dishes. She/he can:

   ♦ Keep the sinks filled with a little soapy water

   ♦ Make sure there are enough dishes to wash

   ♦ Keep the floor dry. (Remember safety.)

   ♦ Talk about who clears the table, and washes and dries the dishes at their homes.

ON STAGE

SET UP

Place

In a corner of the classroom -- Young children feel more secure to be "on stage" if they have walls on at least two sides of them.

Setting

1. Get approximately 24 hollow wooden blocks. Use them to build a 6x4 stage in a corner of your room. Cover the blocks with a rug, or tape them together with wide tape.

2. Get two long boards (6-8 inches wide by 4-6 feet long). They will be "ramps" for entering and exiting the stage. Put one "ramp" on the side of the stage and the other one near a corner of the front of the stage.

72

PROPS

Several hand-held and/or floor
   microphones
Posters to hang on the wall
Instruments
Streamers
Play video camera

PREPARATION

1. Make Microphones

You'll Need
Dowel rods or paper towel rolls
Styrofoam balls

To Make: Push the balls onto the
rods/rolls.

2. Make Shakers

You'll Need
Newspaper
Colored streamers
Tape/Glue

To Make: For each shaker handle, roll
up several pieces of newspaper into a
tube. Cut the streamers into 12"- 18"
lengths. Tape or glue the streamers to
one end of the handle.

3. Get Posters

Good sources for posters are:
Music stores
Travel agencies
Book stores
Education conferences

Look for posters which portray:
Specific topics
Instruments
Actors performing on stage

CLOTHES

(Remember Safety: Be sure none of the clothes
are too long.)

Large scarves
Floppy hats
Beads and necklaces
Fancy jackets
Decorative vests

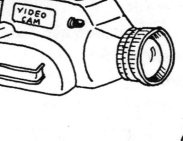

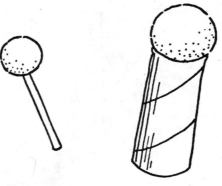

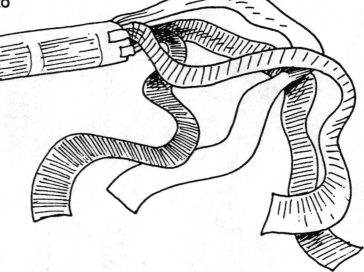

73

PLAY OPPORTUNITIES

1. **Simple Stories.** Have an adult tell the children a story with which they are already familiar, such as THE THREE BILLY GOATS GRUFF. As the adult tells the story, the children can do the actions they want, such as *"Tramp, tramp, tramp"* over the bridge.

2. **Favorite Songs.** Let an adult sing favorite songs with the children. They can act out the song as they sing. Here is a list many children like:

   ♦ *Wheels On the Bus*

   ♦ *Head, Shoulders, Knees, and Toes*

   ♦ *Old McDonald Had a Farm*

   ♦ *Hokey Pokey*

   ♦ *Ring Around the Rosie*

3. **Pre-Recorded Music.** Play music for the children to dance to. (Use the radio, records, tapes, and CD's) This is a good opportunity to bring out the scarves and the shakers. (Have enough room between the children.) Let the children wave them up high and down low -- fast and slow -- in front and back of them. Remember to play a variety of music, such as:

   ♦ Popular dance tunes
   ♦ Classical music -- *Waltz of the Sugarplum Fairy*, etc.
   ♦ Reggae
   ♦ Marches
   ♦ Instrumental and voice
   ♦ Live music -- an adult who plays an instrument such as a guitar, xylophone, or autoharp.

4. **Audience claps** for the people on the stage and sings along with songs they know.

5. **Camera person/s** takes videos of the performers as they sing, play, and act.

6. **Adult** "encourages" the play and helps the children feel comfortable on stage. She/he can:

   ♦ Lead the songs
   ♦ Tell the stories
   ♦ Hand-out the props
   ♦ Make sure that the clothes are worn safely
   ♦ Turn on and off the music
   ♦ Etc.

PICNIC

— SET UP —

Place

In the block area or in a little travelled space of your outside play area.

Inside Setting

Lay a large blanket on the floor with a picnic tablecloth on top of it.

Outside Setting

Have a picnic table with small chairs and/or picnic benches. Put a cloth on the table.

PROPS

Picnic tablecloth
Several small picnic baskets
Picnic supplies
♦ Plates
♦ Paper plate holders
♦ Plastic forks and spoons
♦ Napkins
♦ Lots of plastic food
♦ Small ketchup and mustard bottles
♦ Cups
Portable radio
"Toy" grill
Grill utensils
Grill foods such as hamburgers, hot
    dogs, and sweet corn
Coolers
Plastic soda bottles
Cameras

CLOTHES

Sunglasses
Sun hats
Sun visors (See visor pattern on page 26)
Baseball caps
Backpacks
Mitts for grilling
Aprons for grilling
Chef hats

PREPARATION

None

77

PLAY OPPORTUNITIES

1. **Pack the Picnic Baskets.** Have the picnic supplies and food on the shelves along with picnic baskets and backpacks. Let the children pack and unpack the baskets/backpacks, filling them with the picnic goodies.

2. **Picnic Time.** The picnickers can:

   ♦ Walk to the picnic area, carrying their picnic baskets and supplies. Spread out the table cloth and sit down

   ♦ Unpack the picnic baskets

   ♦ Set the picnic table and pass out the food

   ♦ Eat their picnic -- Delicious!

3. **Picnic Drink.** Fill a thermos jug with cold water. Let several children carry it outside with lots of disposal cups and the picnic table cloth. Spread out the table cloth and put the water and glasses on it. When children get thirsty, sit around the cloth and have a cooling picnic drink.

4. **"Fire-Up" the Grill.** Set the grill outside in the picnic area. Have the grilling utensils, foods, and clothes along with the other basic picnic supplies. Let the children wear their chef aprons and hats, and then "put on the sweet corn," "flip the burgers," and "turn the hot dogs." Have someone call out, *"Time to eat!! Everyone come!"*

5. **Adult** "encourages" the picnic play by:

   ♦ Helping the picnickers unfold and fold their picnic blanket and tablecloth

   ♦ Helping the picnickers pack the picnic goodies into the baskets/backpacks

   ♦ Talking about picnic games and foods

   ♦ Helping the picnickers set the table

   ♦ Pouring picnic drinks

   ♦ "Grilling" the food.

RANCHERS

SET UP

Place

In the block area or adjacent to it.

Setting

1. Build a campfire in the middle of the play area. Roll up sheets of newspaper into long and short tubes or use different length cardboard tubes. Build the campfire with the "logs."

2. Get several rocking and/or spring-loaded horses. Place them around the edges of the area.

3. Have a saddle for children to get on and off. Get two large blocks and a real saddle or a small, heavy blanket. Stack the blocks and tape them together. Put the saddle or heavy blanket over the blocks.

4. Put hay in the water table. Place miniature horses in the hay.

PROPS

Empty food cans
Mixing spoons
Cooking pots
Plates
Cups

Saddle bags with blankets and
    food in the pockets
Stirrups
Shoe shine brushes
Posters
Sleeping bags

CLOTHES

Cowboy hats
Mexican sombreros
Neckerchiefs
Boots
Chaps
Flannel shirts

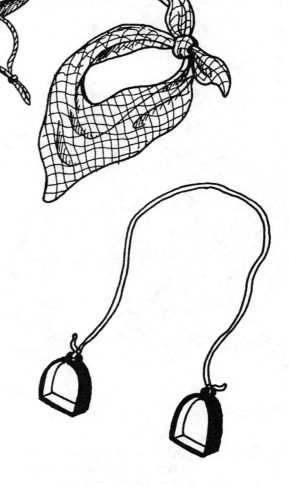

PREPARATION

1. Tie Neckerchiefs

Leave the neckerchiefs tied, so that children can easily put them on and take them off.

2. Secure The Stirrups

You'll Need

Stirrups

Piece of rope long enough to drape over the stack of blocks and touch the floor on both sides.

To Make: Tie a stirrup to each end of the rope. Put the stirrups over the stack of blocks. (Make sure that the stirrups just touch the floor. If not adjust them.) Firmly tape the rope to the blocks. Put the real saddle or heavy blanket over the blocks.

3. Get Western Music

Get western music and play it in the background as the children use the dramatic play area.

4. Get Posters

Good sources for posters are:

Western stores
Travel agencies
Museums

Look for posters which portray:

Horses
Large ranches
Herds of cows

Desert
Farms
People riding horses

PLAY OPPORTUNITIES

1. **Play Around the Campfire.** The "campfire" suggests many types of play. For example:

   ♦ Children can slip into the sleeping bags and "sleep" after a hard day on the ranch.

   ♦ Get out the pots and spoons and let the children "cook" over the fire. One of their favorite things to do is stir, so encourage well-stirred food.

   ♦ Let the children set the cans of food on the fire. Remind the children to use smaller spoons to stir up this food.

   ♦ Eat around the campfire.

   ♦ Sing favorite songs around the campfire.

2. **Feed the Horses.** Have the children put hay in dish tubs and bring it over for the horses to eat. Give the horses carrots for treats.

3. **Brush the Horses.** Let the children "groom" the horses by brushing them with the shoe-shine brushes.

4. Ride the Horses.

♦ As the children are riding the horses, sing GITTY-UP over and over again. You can encourage them to ride faster and slower by the speed at which you sing.

GITTY-UP

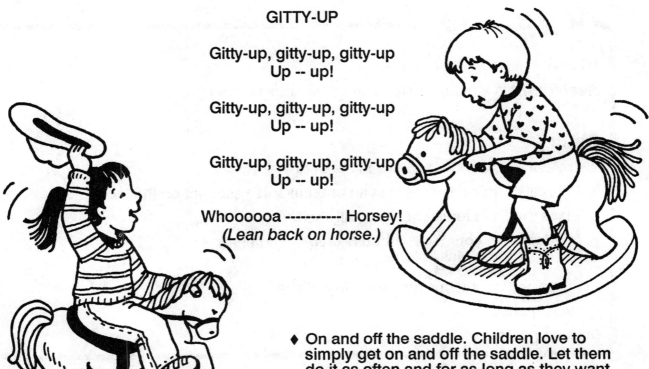

Gitty-up, gitty-up, gitty-up
Up -- up!

Gitty-up, gitty-up, gitty-up
Up -- up!

Gitty-up, gitty-up, gitty-up
Up -- up!

Whoooooa ----------- Horsey!
(Lean back on horse.)

♦ On and off the saddle. Children love to simply get on and off the saddle. Let them do it as often and for as long as they want.

5. **Adult** "encourages" the play and helps the children get involved with the props. She/he can:

   ♦ Lead the songs

   ♦ Help build the campfire

   ♦ Cook with the children

   ♦ Help get the hay for the horses

   ♦ Etc.

RESTAURANT

SET UP

Place

Restaurant is a natural extension of the housekeeping area.

Setting

1. Lay a tablecloth on the table in the area.

2. Put real or artificial flowers in an unbreakable vase. Set on the table.

3. Place the cash register on a small shelf.

4. In addition to your regular housekeeping materials, add:
    - More plastic food
    - Serving trays
    - Several bus tubs for "dirty" dishes

5. Have menus.

6. Hang posters.

PROPS

Posters
Menus
Lots of plastic food
Basic cooking utensils
Order pad and pencil
Tablecloth
Plates
Centerpiece
Bus tub
Mustard/ketchup containers
Unbreakable trays
Cash register
Play money

CLOTHES

Waiter/waitress hats
Aprons
Purses
Wallets
Oven mitts
Rubber gloves

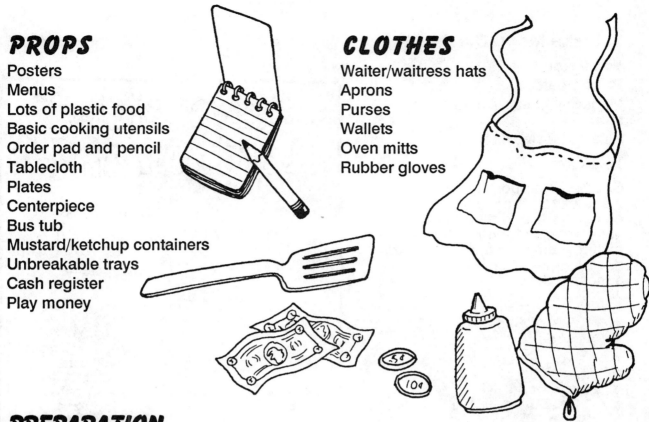

PREPARATION

1. Prepare Food Plates

You'll Need

Heavy-duty disposable plates

Magazine pictures of nutritious foods eaten at breakfast, lunch, and dinner. (Remember to include ethnic foods.)

Clear adhesive paper

To Make:

Use the food pictures to arrange nutritious meals on different plates. Glue each one to its plate and then cover the food with a piece of clear adhesive paper.

85

2. Make Menu Cards

You'll Need
Posterboard
Magazine pictures of nutritious food
Clear adhesive paper

To Make:

Cut the posterboard into 9"x12" menu cards. Glue food pictures on each one and then print the name of each food next to its picture. Laminate the menu cards or cover them with clean adhesive paper.

3. Get Posters

Good sources for posters are:
Grocery stores
Restaurants
Food manufacturers
Milk Council
Food and Drug Administration

Look for posters which portray:
Each category of food
Food triangle
Specific foods such as a salad, serving of spaghetti, bread, etc.

PLAY OPPORTUNITIES

1. **Eat at the Restaurant.** Eating out for breakfast, lunch, or dinner suggests many types of play:

   ♦ "Read" the menu and tell the wait staff what you want.

   ♦ Eat the food and talk to each other.

   ♦ Pay the bill.

2. **Take Food Orders.** Have the waiters and waitresses put on their hats and aprons/smocks. Be sure there are order pads and pencils nearby. The waiters and waitresses can:

   ♦ Set the table
   ♦ Write down the orders
   ♦ Put the food on trays and serve it
   ♦ Clear the dishes and put them in bus tubs.

   HINT: The children like to take orders and serve food to adults. Oftentimes several children are waiting on one adult.

3. **Wash Dishes.** Put your water table near the restaurant. Fill it about half full of water. Add a little soap. Have sponges, dish brushes, and towels. Help the children put the dirty dishes in bus tubs, carry them to the water table sink, wash and dry them, and then put them back in the kitchen cabinets.

4. **Cook Food.** Have lots of plastic food, several extra pots, and additional spatulas, mixing spoons, and pancake turners. Encourage the children to cook different foods by ordering different things, such as:

   ♦ Just order a drink so children can "pour" from a pitcher or coffee pot.

   ♦ Order fresh-baked cookies. Encourage the children to wear oven mitts and put the cookies on a cookie sheet and bake them in the oven. "*Oh they smell so good!*" When finished take them off the cookie sheet and serve them.

   ♦ Order soup which the children can stir in the pot before serving it to you.

5. **Walk to the Ice Cream Shop.** Call ahead and make arrangements to go to your local ice cream shop. Let the children each order an ice cream cone. Eat them at the picnic spot outside the shop or sit at tables inside. After everyone is finished, "wash-up" with disposable wipes.

6. **Adult** "encourages" the play at the restaurant by:
   ♦ Ordering food
   ♦ Talking while eating
   ♦ Putting dishes back in the cabinet after they've been washed.

7. "Drive-Up" Window

In an open area of the classroom set up a "drive-up" window. Each time you do this, focus on one type of restaurant such as pizza, chicken, hot dogs, hamburgers, etc. Get props to go along with that food and restaurant.

HINT: Fast food restaurants can usually donate, loan, or inexpensively sell signs, props, and supplies. They may also have outdated caps and uniforms which the staff no longer wears.

1. Put a puppet stage in the middle of the open area.

2. Tape a restaurant sign to the top of the puppet stage.

3. Use masking tape to build a road leading up to the window. Have a stop sign along the road for the customers to stop and order.

4. Put the food, containers, and bags on the shelves of the puppet stage.

5. Have riding toys available.

SHOE STORE

Place

In the housekeeping area or space adjacent to it.

Setting

1. Put several chairs side by side or two low benches back to back in the open space.

2. Lay a full-length mirror on its side in an open space near the chairs.

3. Line up a variety of shoes, boots, and slippers on a low shelf or the floor.

4. Have a "check-out" table with cash registers and calculators on it. Set shoe boxes and bags under the table or on a shelf near the table.

PROPS

Shoe boxes with lids
Plastic or paper bags with handles
Several cash registers
Several calculators
Purses
Wallets
Foot measurers
Lacing boards
Baby dolls
Empty shoe polish containers
Shoe polish brushes

CLOTHES

Different footwear, including some for babies
(Remember Safety: Loosely lace the footwear that has laces.)

Vests
Ties
Hats
Necklaces

PREPARATION

1. Make Several Foot Measurers

You'll Need
Corrugated cardboard
Wide colored tape
Wide and narrow marker
Ruler

To Make:
1) Cut the corrugated cardboard into 7"x9" pieces.
2) Place a strip of colored tape along the left side of each board.
3) Use the narrow marker to draw-in and number the inches on each tape.
4) Use the wide marker to draw a foot shape on each board.

2. Make Several Lacing Boards

You'll Need
Corrugated cardboard
Long shoe lace for each lacing board
Tape

To Make:
1) Cut the corrugated board into 6"x 8" pieces.
2) Draw a shoe shape on each board and punch holes.
3) Attach the lace to the board:
   - Insert one end of the lace into the board from the bottomside and pull it almost halfway through.
   - Tie a large knot in the lace on each side of the board to secure it. Add tape on the bottomside if necessary.
   - Pull the other end of the lace through matching hole.

91

FOOT MEASURER

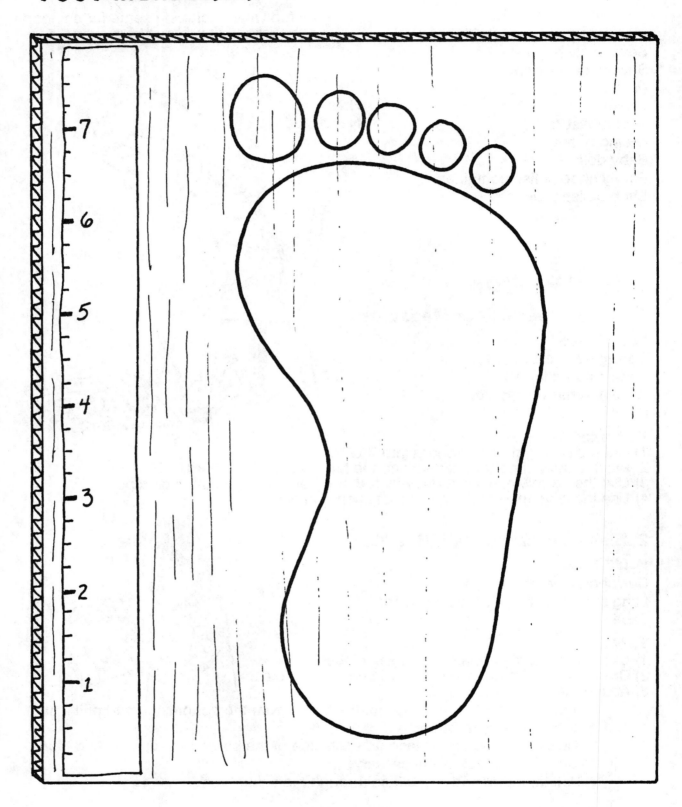

LACING BOARD

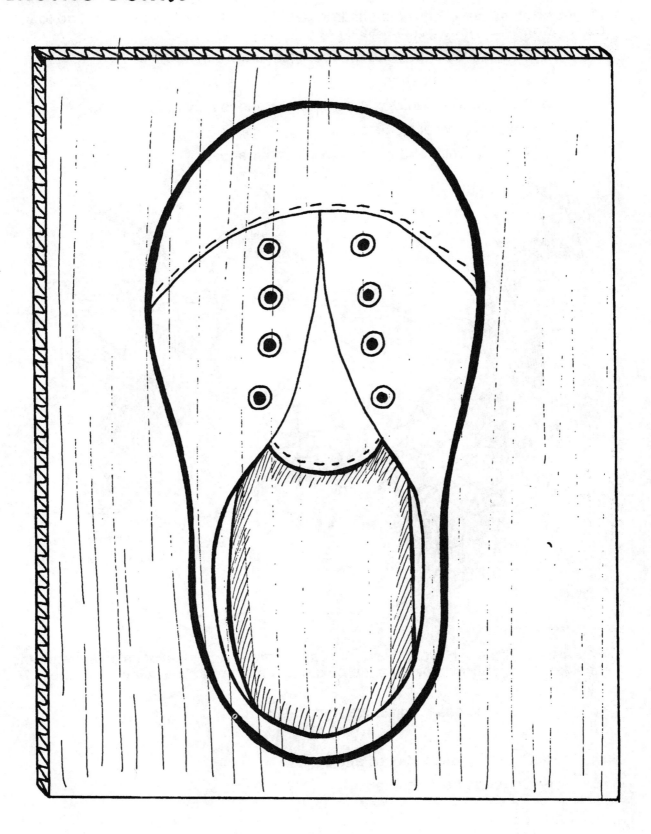

PLAY OPPORTUNITIES

1. Buying New Shoes. Have the children get their wallets and purses and go to the shoe store. When they get there they can:

♦ Measure their feet with the foot measurers

♦ Try on different shoes, boots, and slippers

♦ Walk along the mirror, looking at the shoes they are trying on

♦ Help each other try on shoes

♦ Put on jewelry and hats to go with their shoes.

2. Pay for the Shoes. Have at least one cash register and several calculators on the "check-out" table. Have lots of shoe boxes and bags readily available. Let the children:

♦ Work the cash registers and calculators

♦ Pay for the shoes

♦ Put the shoes in boxes and bags

♦ Carry the bags "home"

3. **Buy New Shoes for the Babies.** Put the dolls and a variety of baby shoes and boots in the area. Let the children be the moms and dads and help their babies buy new shoes, boots, and slippers.

4. **Lace Up the Shoes.** Put out pairs of shoes/boots that need lacing. When children come to the shoe store that day, they can buy shoes and boots that have laces. While they are trying on the shoes/boots, help them lace, unlace, and tie.

EXTENSION: Put the "Lacing Boards" on a shelf in the housekeeping area for children to use.

5. **Polish the Shoes.** Put the shoe polish containers and shoe brushes in the shoe store. Let the shoe store workers polish and shine the shoes/boots before the store opens.

6. **Adult** "encourages" the play and helps the children get involved with buying, selling, and caring for shoes by:

   ♦ Talking with customers about new shoes

   ♦ Measuring and helping customers try on new footwear

   ♦ Being a parent taking his/her children to the shoe store

   ♦ Boxing and bagging the shoes someone has bought

   ♦ Polishing/shining footwear.

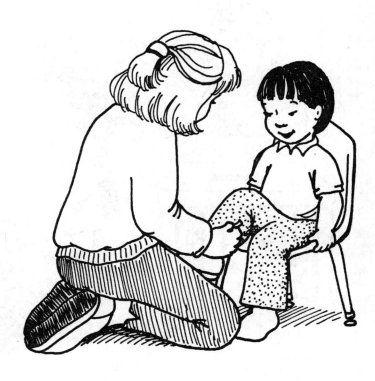

TRANSPORTATION

SET UP

Place

In an open area of the classroom, near a wall.

Setting

1. Make a simple gas pump. Get a tall box and cover it with plain paper. Draw details on it with colored markers. Cut a small hole in the side and slip a long piece of hose in it.

2. Set up the GAS STATION STORE. Have a table with a cash register. Next to the table have a shelf with empty milk cartons, soda bottles, and empty cracker boxes.

3. Construct a parking lot for all the vehicles. First tape off the whole gas station area with wide colored tape. Then use a different color of tape to make parking spaces for the different vehicles.

4. Build the roads. Use tape to make a road which starts at the gas station, winds through the classroom, and then comes back to the gas station.

PROPS

Riding vehicles such as cars, trucks, wagons, bikes, etc.
Driving bench
Traffic signs, especially a stop sign
Car seats
Stuffed animals
Large dolls
Baby dolls
Baby blankets
Old keys on rings
Cash register
Traffic tickets

CLOTHES

Headbands/visors/hats for the gas station attendants, bus drivers, and train engineers
Smocks
Purses

PREPARATION

1. Make Cardboard Vehicles
(to supplement your riding toys)

You'll Need
Sturdy boxes large enough for one child plus her supplies
Sturdy styrofoam plates
Brads

To Make Each Vehicle:

1) Cover each box with appropriate paper or paint.

2) Draw two wheels on the sides of each box.

3) Make the "steering wheels" by loosely attaching a plate with a brad to the inside front sides of each box.

4) Cut a slit near the steering wheel for the children to put their keys in.

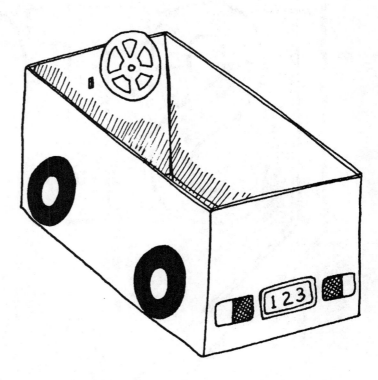

2. Make Buses And Trains

You'll Need
Lots of chairs

To Make: Line up the chairs in a single or double row

3. Make A Hand-held Stop Sign

You'll Need
Red construction paper
Paint stir stick

To Make: Use the "stop" pattern to make your sign. Cut it out and glue it to the stir stick.

4. Make Headbands

You'll Need
Posterboard
Colored markers

To Make: Cut bands out to fit your children's heads. Duplicate the worker signs, color them, and staple them to the bands

PLAY OPPORTUNITIES

1. **Drive Around**. Let the children "drive" the vehicles along the road you built.

   ♦ Let the children start their cars and trucks with keys. While they are driving they can hang their keys on the handle bars. If they are using the cardboard vehicles, they can stick the keys in the slits.

   ♦ An adult can be a traffic officer with a stop sign. Let the children "drive" until they see you. They should stop and then proceed when you say it is safe.
   HINT: This type of play also helps the children "drive" at a safe pace.

   ♦ Encourage the children to make the noises of their vehicles as they drive. They can be horns, brakes, sirens, engines, radios, etc.

2. **Too Fast!** An adult can put on a police hat/headband and "stop" drivers who are going too fast. They can:

   ♦ Talk to the drivers about safe driving.

   ♦ Give the drivers speeding tickets.

3. **Take the Babies for a Drive**. Let the children put the stuffed animals, babies, and dolls in the vehicles and take them for a ride. The children can:

   ♦ Use belts for seatbelts.

   ♦ Use car seats for the babies. Remember to take the baby blankets in case the babies get cold.

   ♦ Put the dolls in a wagon and take them for a walk.

4. **Pay the Toll**. Let an adult sit along the road and be a toll booth collector. The children come up to the toll booth, give the attendant a "Hi-5" and then drive on. The attendant might talk to the drivers:

   ♦ Where they are going.

   ♦ What kind of car they are driving.

   ♦ Who else is in the car.

   ♦ Remind them to drive slowly and safely.

5. **Gas Up**. Let the drivers pull up to the gas pump and tell the station attendant what they want. The attendant can fill the vehicle with gas, wash the windows, check the engine, take the money, etc.

6. **Buy Milk**. Let the children come into the "gas station store" and "buy" what their families need.

7. **All Aboard**. Let the chairs become a train or bus. Have car seats on some of the chairs for the babies and belts on the chairs for seat belts. Have the adult put on his hat/headband and help the passengers

   ♦ Bump up and down
   ♦ Sing songs
   ♦ Talk about where they're going
   ♦ Rock the babies
   ♦ Make vehicle noises
   ♦ And so on.

8. **Adult** "encourages" the play as she/he pretends to be the:
   ♦ Traffic officer
   ♦ Police officer
   ♦ Toll booth collector
   ♦ Gas station attendant
   ♦ Gas station store clerk
   ♦ Bus driver or train engineer

TRIPS AND VACATIONS

SET UP

Place

In an open space in the room or as an expansion of the housekeeping area.

Setting

1. Put 8-10 chairs in a double line to make a train, bus, or airplane.

2. Set several suitcases, clothes, and travel accessories on a shelf. You may want this special shelf in the open area near your vehicle, or use one that is already in your housekeeping area. Keep in mind that housekeeping is a very natural place to have suitcases, clothes, and travel accessories.

3. Put vacation albums and scrapbooks on the book shelf.

4. Hang travel posters on the walls.

PROPS

Several steering wheels
Suitcases
Overnight bags
Posters
Tickets to board
Cameras
Vacation albums and scrapbooks
Post cards
Travel-size shampoo bottles, soaps, etc.
Hair brushes
Empty toothpaste containers

CLOTHES

All types of clothes to pack, such as:
♦ Shorts
♦ Swim suits
♦ Pajamas
♦ Dresses
♦ Shoes
♦ Blue jeans
♦ Purses
Pilot, train engineer, and bus driver hats

PREPARATION

1. Get Posters

Good sources for posters are:
Travel agencies
Transportation companies
Campsites
Amusement parks

Look for posters which portray:
Camping
Vacation spots
Beaches
Amusement parks
Zoos
Airports
Airplanes
Trains
Buses
Campers

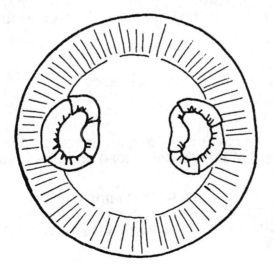

2. Make Paper Plate Steering Wheels

Get several very sturdy paper plates. Cut a kidney-shaped hole, large enough for the children's hands to fit into, on two sides of each plate. Reinforce the two holes with tape.

PLAY OPPORTUNITIES

1. **All Aboard.** Have someone get a steering wheel and put on the driver, pilot, or engineer hat. The children can:

♦ Give their tickets to the driver and then board

♦ Carry their luggage with them

♦ Sing songs while they travel

♦ Talk about where they are going, who they are visiting, and what they are going to do

♦ Make honking, whistling, and chugging noises as they travel.

2. **Eating on Vacation.**

♦ Have a blanket, stop along the way, and eat your picnic lunch.

♦ Stop at your favorite fast food restaurant and eat.

♦ Eat while you are riding on the airplane, bus, or train.

3. **Packing and Unpacking Clothes.**

♦ Put several types of suitcases and overnight bags on the shelf, along with lots of clothes and travel accessories. Let the children pack the clothes they will need for their trip. As they are packing talk about:

- Where they are going
- Who they will visit
- What clothes they are putting in their suitcases
- The posters on the wall
- Who is going with them.

♦ Have 4-5 suitcases with different closures -- long and short zippers, snaps, clips, locks, velcro, etc. Let the children close and open the suitcases.

♦ When the children "return" from their trips let them unpack their suitcases and put the clothes and accessories back on the shelf. As they are unpacking, talk about their clothes, the people they saw, the places they went, and the food they ate.

4. **Sing Songs on the Trip.** While driving along, sing everyone's favorite songs. Begin with *Happy Birthday*, *The Wheels On the Bus*, and *London Bridges*. Let the children choose more songs.

5. **Carry the Suitcases.** Have several wagons and riding vehicles. Let the children pack their suitcases and carry them to the "car." Wave good-bye to the travellers and let them "drive" off. When they return they can carry their suitcases back to the house.

6. **Adults:**

   ♦ Need to be sensitive to the travel experiences children have had, so the conversation, packing, and actual travel is relevant to the types of trips they have taken.

   ♦ Can set up "Vacation" play several days before he/she is actually going on a trip. This will help the children realize that their teacher will not be there for several days. It will also let the children know that their teacher is having a good time, where she/he is, and that she/he is coming back to see them.

   ♦ Can "encourage" the play while:

     - Driving the bus, train, or airplane
     - Unpacking the picnic lunch or being the server at the fast food restaurant
     - Helping the children get ready for their trips
     - Singing
     - Talking with the children about the pictures in the vacation albums and on the posters and post cards.

BOOK LIST

Compiled by Jeanne Lybecker
Early Childhood Consultant
Beaverton, Oregon

AT THE BEACH

- *At the Beach* by Anne Rockwell, illustrated by Harlow Rockwell, Macmillan, 1987
- *Joshua By the Sea* by Angela Johnson, illustrated by Rhonda Mitchell, Orchard, 1994
- *On the Beach: What Can You Find?* Dorling Kindersley, 1993
- *Tom and Pippo On the Beach* by Helen Oxenbury, Candlewick, 1993

BABY

- *Baby's Book of Babies,* The by Kathy Henderson, Puffin, 1993
- *Here Come the Babies* by Catherine and Laurence Anholt, Candlewick, 1993
- *I'm a Baby, You're a Baby* by Lisa Kopper, Viking, 1995
- *Look, Baby! Listen, Baby! Do, Baby!* by True Kelley, Dutton, 1987
- *Where's the Baby?* by Tom Paxton, illustrated by Mark Graham, Morrow, 1993

CAMPING

- *Bailey Goes Camping* by Kevin Henkes, Puffin, 1989
- *Just Me and My Dad* by Mercer Mayer, Western, 1977

CONSTRUCTION

- *Diggers* by Mathew Price, illustrated by Paul Strickland, Dutton, 1993
- *Building a House* by Byron Barton, Mulberry, 1990
- *Machines at Work* by Byron Barton, Harper, 1987
- *Road Builders* by B.G. Hennessy, illustrated by Simms Taback, Viking, 1994

DOCTOR

- *Corduroy Goes To the Doctor* by Lisa McCue, Viking, 1987
- *Going To the Doctor* by Fred Rodgers, Putnam, 1986
- *My Dentist* by Harlow Rockwell, Macmillan, 1987
- *My Doctor* by Harlow Rockwell, Macmillan, 1992

FIRE FIGHTERS

- *All About Fire Trucks* by Teddy Slater, Putnam, 1991
- *Fire Engines* by Anne Rockwell, Dutton, 1986
- *Fireman Small* by Wong Herbert Yee, Houghton Mifflin, 1994
- *Clifford the Firehouse Dog* by Norman Bridwell, Scholastic, 1994

GROCERY STORE

- *Don't Forget the Bacon!* by Pat Hutchins, Morrow, 1989
- *Supermarket, The* by Anne Rockwell, Macmillan, 1979
- *When We Go Shopping* by Nick Butterworth, Little Brown, 1994

HAIR STYLIST

- *Michael's New Haircut* by Karen Frandsen, Children's Press, 1986

HAPPY BIRTHDAY

- *Don't Wake Up Mama!* by Eileen Christelow, Houghton Mifflin, 1992
- *Happy Birthday, Moon* by Frank Asch, Simon and Schuster, 1988
- *Happy Birthday to Me* by Anne Rockwell, Macmillan, 1981
- *It's My Birthday* by Helen Oxenbury, Candlewick, 1994
- *Max's Birthday* by Rosemary Wells, Dial, 1985

HOUSEKEEPING

BAKING AND COOKING

♦ *Benny Bakes a Cake* by Eve Rice, Mulberry, 1993

♦ *Cake That Mack Ate* by R. Robart, illustrated by M. Kovalski, Little Brown, 1991

♦ *Mr. Cookie Baker* by Monica Wellington, Dutton, 1992

♦ *Spot Bakes a Cake* by Eric Hill, Putnam, 1994

CARE FOR THE PETS

♦ *Dog, The* by John Burningham, Candlewick, 1995

♦ *Lizzie and Her Puppy* by David Martin, illustrated by Debi Glori, Candlewick, 1993

♦ *My Fuzzy Friends* by Elizabeth Hathon, Grosset and Dunlap, 1993

♦ *Pretend You're a Cat* by Jean Marzollo, illustrated by Jerry Pinkney, Dutton, 1990

CLEAN-UP

♦ *Clean-up Day* by Kate Duke, Dutton, 1986

♦ *When There's Work To Do* by Nick Butterworth, Little Brown, 1994

♦ *Willie's Boot* by Martha Alexander, Candlewick, 1993

DO THE LAUNDRY

♦ *Pocket for Corduroy, A* by Don Freeman, Puffin, 1989

♦ *Tom & Pippo & the Washing Machine* by Helen Oxenbury, Macmillan, 1988

GET DRESSED-UP

♦ *Carl's Masquerade* by Alexandra Day, FS & G, 1993

♦ *Martin's Hats* by Joan Blos, Mulberry, 1984

♦ *Spot Goes To a Party* Eric Hill, Putnam, 1992

HOUSEKEEPING (CONT.)

WASH THE DISHES

- *My Kitchen* by Harlow Rockwell, Greenwillow, 1980
- *Pots and Pans* by Anne Rockwell, illustrated by Lizzy Rockwell, Macmillan, 1993

ON STAGE

- *Clap Your Hands* by Lorinda Bryan Cauley, Putnam, 1992
- *Color Dance* by Ann Jonas, Greenwillow, 1989
- *One Ballerina Two* by Vivian French, illustrated Jan Omerod, Lothrop, 1991

PICNIC

- *Nicky's Picnic* by Harriet Ziefert, illustrated Richard Brown, Puffin, 1986
- *Picnic* by Emily Arnold McCully, Harper, 1989
- *Teddy Bears' Picnic, The* by Renate Kozikowski, 1990
- *Yum! Yum!* by Clara Vulliamy, Candlewick, 1994

RESTAURANT

- *Benjy Goes To a Restaurant* by Jill Krementz, Crown 1986
- *Eating Out* by Helen Oxenbury, Dial, 1983
- *Sheep Out to Eat* by Nancy Shaw, illustrated by Margot Apple, Houghton Mifflin, 1992

SHOE STORE

- *New Blue Shoes* by Eve Rice, Macmillan, 1975
- *Shoes* by Elizabeth Winthrop, Harper, 1988
- *Two New Sneakers* by Nancy Tafuri, Greenwillow, 1988
- *Two Shoes, New Shoes* by Shirley Hughes, Lothrop, 1986

TRANSPORTATION

- *Airplanes* by Byron Barton, Harper, 1986
- *Airport* by Byron Barton, Harper, 1987
- *Big Book of Things That Go*, The by Dorling Kindersley, 1994
- *Freight Train* by Donald Crews, Mulberry, 1992
- *Planes* by Anne Rockwell, Puffin, 1994
- *Trains* by Byron Barton, Harper, 1994
- *Trains* by Anne Rockwell, Puffin, 1992
- *Wheels On the Bus, The* by Paul Zelinsky, Dutton, 1990

TRIPS AND VACATIONS

- *Car Trip, The* by Helen Oxenbury, Dial, 1983
- *Clifford Takes a Trip* by Norman Bridwell, Scholastic, 1985
- *Emma's Vacation* by David McPhail, Dutton, 1987
- *On Our Vacation* by Anne Rockwell, Dutton, 1989
- *Our Puppy's Vacation* by Ruth Brown, Unicorn, 1991

BUILDING BLOCKS Library

The Circle Time Series

by Liz and Dick Wilmes. Hundreds of activities for large and small groups of children. Each book is filled with Language and Active games, Fingerplays, Songs, Stories, Snacks, and more. A great resource for every library shelf.

Circle Time Book
Captures the spirit of 39 holidays and seasons.
ISBN 0-943452-00-7   **$ 12.95**

Everyday Circle Times
Over 900 ideas. Choose from 48 topics divided into 7 sections: self-concept, basic concepts, animals, foods, science, occupations, and recreation.
ISBN 0-943452-01-5   **$16.95**

More Everyday Circle Times
Divided into the same 7 sections as EVERYDAY. Features new topics such as Birds and Pizza, plus all new ideas for some familiar topics contained in EVERYDAY.
ISBN 0-943452-14-7   **$16.95**

Yearful of Circle Times
52 different topics to use weekly, by seasons, or mixed throughout the year. New Friends, Signs of Fall, Snowfolk Fun, and much more.
ISBN 0-943452-10-4   **$16.95**

Paint Without Brushes

by Liz and Dick Wilmes. Use common materials which you already have. Discover the painting possibilities in your classroom! PAINT WITHOUT BRUSHES gives your children open-ended art activities to explore paint in lots of creative ways. A valuable art resource. One you'll want to use daily.
ISBN 0-943452-15-5   **$12.95**

Gifts, Cards, and Wraps

by Wilmes and Zavodsky. Help the children sparkle with the excitement of gift giving. Filled with thoughtful gifts, unique wraps, and special cards which the children can make and give. They're sure to bring smiles.
ISBN 0-943452-06-6   **$ 7.95**

Everyday Bulletin Boards

by Wilmes and Moehling. Features borders, murals, backgrounds, and other open-ended art to display on your bulletin boards. Plus board ideas with patterns, which teachers can make and use to enhance their curriculum.
ISBN 0-943452-09-0   **$ 12.95**

Exploring Art

by Liz and Dick Wilmes. EXPLORING ART is divided by months. Over 250 art ideas for paint, chalk, doughs, scissors, and more. Easy to set-up in your classroom.
ISBN 0-943452-05-8   **$19.95**

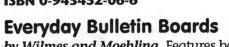

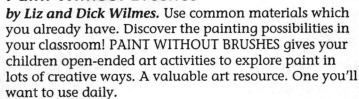

2's Experience Series

by Liz and Dick Wilmes. An exciting series developed especially for toddlers and two's.

2's Experience Art

Art for toddlers and two's! Over 150 activities... Scribble, Paint, Smear, Mix, Tear, Mold, Paste, and more. Plus lots of recipes and hints.
ISBN 0-943452-21-X   **$ 16.95**

2's Experience Dramatic Play

Dress up and pretend! Let toddlers and two's play hundreds of imaginary characters... firefighters, campers, bus drivers, and more.
ISBN 0-943452-20-1   **$12.95**

2's Experience Felt Board Fun

Hundreds of extra large patterns accompany special stories, rhymes, and activities... teddy bears, birthdays, farm animals, and more.
ISBN 0-943452-19-8   **$14.95**

2's Experience Fingerplays

Wonderful collection of easy fingerplays with accompanying games and large FINGERPLAY CARDS— illustrations for one side and words/movement for the other..
ISBN 0-943452-18-X   **$12.95**

Learning Centers

by Liz and Dick Wilmes. Hundreds of open-ended activities to quickly involve and excite your children. You'll use it every time you plan and whenever you need a quick, additional activity. A must for every teacher's bookshelf.
ISBN 0-943452-13-9   **$19.95**

Felt Board Fun

by Liz and Dick Wilmes. Make your felt board come alive. Discover how versatile it is as the children become involved with a wide range of activities. This unique book has over 150 ideas with accompanying patterns.
ISBN 0-943452-02-3   **$16.95**

Table & Floor Games

by Liz and Dick Wilmes. 32 easy-to-make, fun-to-play table/floor games with accompanying patterns ready to trace or photocopy. Teach beginning concepts such as matching, counting, colors, alphabet recognition, sorting and so on.
ISBN 0-943452-16-3   **$19.95**

Activities Unlimited

by Adler, Caton, and Cleveland. Create an enthusiasm for learning! Hundreds of innovative activities to help your children develop fine and gross motor skills, increase their language, become self-reliant, and play cooperatively. Whether you're a beginning teacher or a veteran, this book will quickly become one of your favorites.
ISBN 0-943452-17-1   **$16.95**

Parachute Play

by Liz and Dick Wilmes. A year 'round approach to one of the most versatile pieces of large muscle equipment. Starting with basic techniques, PARACHUTE PLAY provides over 100 activities to use with your parachute.

ISBN 0-943452-03-1   **$9.95**

Classroom Parties

by Susan Spaete. Each party plan suggests decorations, trimmings, and snacks which the children can easily make to set a festive mood. Choose from games, songs, art activities, stories, and related experiences which will add to the spirit and fun.

ISBN 0-943452-07-4   **$8.95**

A ll books available from teacher stores, school supply catalogs or directly from:

38W567 Brindlewood
Elgin, Illinois   60123
800-233-2448   708-742-1054 (FAX)

Thank you for your order.

	Each	Total
BUILDING BLOCKS Subscription	20.00	_____
2's EXPERIENCE Series		
2'S EXPERIENCE ART	16.95	_____
2'S EXPERIENCE DRAMATIC PLAY	12.95	_____
2'S EXPERIENCE FELTBOARD FUN	14.95	_____
2'S EXPERIENCE FINGERPLAYS	12.95	_____
CIRCLE TIME Series		
CIRCLE TIME BOOK	12.95	_____
EVERYDAY CIRCLE TIMES	16.95	_____
MORE EVERYDAY CIRCLE TIMES	16.95	_____
YEARFUL OF CIRCLE TIMES	16.95	_____
ACTIVITIES UNLIMITED	16.95	_____
CLASSROOM PARTIES	8.95	_____
EXPLORING ART	19.95	_____
EVERYDAY BULLETIN BOARDS	12.95	_____
FELT BOARD FUN	16.95	_____
GIFTS, CARDS, AND WRAPS	7.95	_____
LEARNING CENTERS	19.95	_____
PAINT WITHOUT BRUSHES	12.95	_____
TABLE & FLOOR GAMES	19.95	_____
PARACHUTE PLAY	9.95	_____
	TOTAL	_____

Name_____

Address _____

City_____

State_____ Zip _____

QUALITY

SINCE 1977